# Praise for The Laney Gwinner Effect

*The Laney Gwinner Effect: How One Cold Case Mobilized a High School to Make a Difference*, a book written by high school teacher Randy Hubbard is a testament to good teachers everywhere. This book follows a Forensic Science teacher who started a class to educate more students in forensics, to re-evaluate cold cases and to give his students a real-world experience along with helping families who were the victims of murder. Randy is educating the future Cold Case and Innocence Project investigators who may not just help to solve a case and bring justice to the victims and surviving family members, but may also help to save a falsely convicted individual from the cruelty of capital punishment by bringing new forensic evidence to the attention of law enforcement and the Courts. As a forensic expert, I recommend this book to everyone interested in truth!

**—Retired Det. Sgt. Kevin Gannon**
Bronx Homicide Task Force/Nightwatch Division

The True Crime genre has a large following, which generates a rich body of books, podcasts and shows to satiate the masses. With such a plethora of sources, it is difficult to imagine someone coming up with an idea that is original and fresh. Randy Hubbard's book, *The Laney Gwinner Effect: How One Cold Case Mobilized a High School to Make a Difference*, is one that actually succeeds in being unique, however, in that it explores a cold case murder through the eyes of a high school class that tried to tackle and achieve what the police could not. Interesting and fresh, this book should be of interest to both True Crime fans and educators looking for innovative ways to inspire their young students.

—**Dr. Mark Godsey**
Author of *Blind Injustice*
Director of the Ohio Innocence Project

Imagine bonding with your teacher over a cold case. Working a case together. Searching for information, evidence and witnesses. The day y'all pinpointed the location of the victim's missing car. At the end of their time together their newfound knowledge led to their class looking into more than 50 cases. Fifty families, fifty crime scenes and fifty detectives. It was a way to use education to bring light to the cold stories and answers to families. This teacher, a life-long educator, learned a lesson himself. This work with the students led him back to his faith because he realized it was no accident that he met that particular student and they picked that particular case. Laney found them. This teacher and these students will forever be bonded by the pursuit of justice.

—**CSI Sheryl "Mac" McCollum, MS**

# THE LANEY GWINNER EFFECT

How One Cold Case Mobilized a High
School to Make a Difference

RANDY HUBBARD

Genius
Book Publishing

**Published by:**
Genius Book Publishing
PO Box 250380
Milwaukee Wisconsin 53225 USA
GeniusBookPublishing.com

ISBN: 978-1-958727-53-9

241217 Trade

# Contents

*This book is dedicated to Alana "Laney" Gwinner.*

*This book is also dedicated to my parents, Ben and Norinne Hubbard. They always taught me to work hard, take chances, and care for others. The goal was to complete this book before they passed away, but unfortunately, I was not able to accomplish that. Thank you, Mom and Dad, for your unconditional love.*

# Introduction

**"The sound of rain needs no translation."**
— Alan Watts

As I sit here on my patio typing up a review of Laney's case to give to the local police, a calm and refreshing rain begins to fall, as though Laney, her parents, her friends, and anyone that knew her are crying for her justice. A tranquil moment, affirming what I am doing right now matters.

Alana Gwinner was known as Laney to her friends and will mostly be referred to as Laney in this book, but to her mother, Alana is the correct way to say her name. When the billboards were placed around town, in Fairfield and Hamilton, Ohio, Mrs. Sandra Gwinner always made sure the police called her Alana. These billboards were put up in places the long-time sheriff's detective Frank Smith thought the killer would see every day. Frank was hoping to put pressure on that person to let them know that they knew he was close by and they would find him. Twenty-five years later, Alana Gwinner's killer still walks among us. This monster has been covered by the darkness, carrying a secret that is undoubtedly eating them alive.

As I sit and watch the rain, I begin to think back on how I got involved with Laney and her story. I did not know Alana Gwinner. I never saw her in person, and I didn't even know her story until twenty years after her passing, but when I began to do research with a student of mine on cold cases, it almost seemed as if she found me.

As a teacher of thirty-two years, you start to look to that day you can walk away into the sunset called retirement. It seems so close but yet so far away at the same time. I have enjoyed every year of my teaching career, but like all individuals when the light is at the end of the tunnel, it starts to get harder to stay focused on the task at hand. I have watched others in the profession just bide their time until they can pack up their belongings and move on to that final phase of their life. Let's face it, time isn't exactly in our favor, but we can choose to enjoy that phase or not, and the choice lies with each individual. I was beginning to feel myself slide into that "let's just make it" mode when Evan Fletcher, a student in my Forensic Science class, sparked an idea. He got me to realize that I needed something to ignite my passion for my job again. Evan was a very curious young man who loved to learn new things. Our discussions in class were always interesting and very thoughtful. One day as we talked about true crime shows we had seen on TV, we challenged each other to do something that would push us to our intellectual limits: We decided to look for our own cold case to research and dive into.

When we started this process with Laney's story, we had no idea how it was going to affect us. It started as a research project, but then it became so much more. We did our initial research, finding news articles, reports, and even a podcast about her story. We looked at maps of where she disappeared and where she was found.

We started writing names on a whiteboard and drawing lines to connect people we wanted to talk to. We drove to the bowling alley where she was last seen and looked at the bar where she had her last drink. As we were sitting there looking around the bowling alley and talking, a man came up to us and asked if he could help us, and we got the guts to ask, "Hey do you know anything about the girl that disappeared from here in 1997?" The dam had been broken. The next four years would bring a deluge of information, crazy stories, and a journey into a case that still has not been solved.

The one thing that I hope Alana Gwinner sees from Heaven above is that her existence here on Earth has had a lasting impact on those she knew and on those she never got to meet. This book is about Alana Gwinner and her awful departure from us, but it is also about how her story opened the eyes of a student and a teacher and has affected them forever. It's the story of how Laney helped start a program in which high school seniors learn the realities of life in hopes of one day bringing peace to a family that has lost a loved one to violent crime.

Alana, you have touched my heart and have given me the passion to keep getting better at my job until the day I walk into the sunset. I promise I will teach my best these final few years because of you. I also promise that I will not stop until your brother and your friends know who took you from them on that fateful night. That monster is still around here, and their demons will one day show themselves.

The rain becomes lighter and the sun now begins to shine…

## "I'm on my way"

**"The Last Words Spoken Echo in the Dark Forever"**
— Randy Hubbard

THE CALM RAIN I was watching from my patio when I started this book is nothing compared to what hit us in 1997. The greater Cincinnati area was hammered by torrential rainstorms that spring. I remember this because my childhood home, which my parents still live in, is less than one hundred feet from the Great Miami River. They had lived in that home for more than forty years, and it had never reached the house before. That March we spent about twenty-four to forty-eight hours moving furniture and watching the water rush through the basement as if the river had decided to take anything in its path. The Ohio River had risen to a record 64.7 feet and had taken over the streets of downtown Cincinnati. Many small towns along the river from Manchester, Ohio, to Louisville, Kentucky, were destroyed like the mythical city of Atlantis.

Maybe the raging river was foreshadowing the cold secrets it would carry later that year.

I had moved away from my hometown of Fairfield, Ohio, about five years earlier to build a life with my wonderful new bride in Kansas City, Kansas. We loved our time in Kansas, but we knew after our first daughter was born in 1996 it was time to return home to be with family. We found a perfect house for us in Burlington, Kentucky. We were back. Back to see the Cincinnati Reds flounder to a 76–86 third-place finish. Back to watch the Bengals miss the playoffs for the seventh year in a row. It was home, and we were so happy to be back.

That year, I started a new teaching position at Harrison High School. I was always proud of being innovative in my classroom. Doing something different to make the classroom more enjoyable for my students was always something I strived to accomplish. Heck, I even talked my principal into letting me take over an old industrial arts room and make a zoo. I guess you could call me the Tiger King of small rodents, reptiles, and birds. As I taught my biology class about the circulatory system and blood, using the relatively new idea of weaving in forensic science, I did not realize an event that would occur on December 10, 1997, would rejuvenate my passion for teaching and helping others after twenty years. It would be the catalyst to open my mind to the intrigue of true crime, new friendships, and professional connections, and, most of all, introduce me to a young woman I would never get to meet in person.

As Forrest Gump said, the 1990s "was like a box of chocolates, you never know what you're gonna get." It was the era of boy bands and the Harry Potter series. Y2K signified the world's end in the year 2000, and music icon Prince wanted us all to "party like it was 1999." On the world stage, the Oklahoma City bomber, Timothy McVeigh, got his well-deserved sentence of death from the courts, while in that same month, the world lost a true princess with the awful death of Princess Diana. Here in the Cincinnati area, towns were starting to put the pieces back together from the damage caused by the rising rivers earlier that year. The city was actively trying to improve its highways. The city council even talked about building a light rail to move people along the I-71 corridor to improve business ventures. Now we know how government projects work. It is twenty-five years later, there is no light rail, and the I-71/I-75 roadwork seems to never end.

Despite the endless construction zone of doom, Cincinnati and the surrounding areas were really progressing back then to make this part of Ohio a place that would attract more people. Things seemed to be going well, but like all cities, big and small, there are always underlying stories of tragedy. On December 5, 1997, the Cincinnati Police Department was rocked by the sudden loss of Officers Ronald Jeter and Daniel Pope. An individual they were serving a warrant to ambushed the two highly decorated officers, killing them both with gunshot wounds to the head. This story hit hard on the emotions of this town that seemed to be changing its reputation as a rough place to be.

These were the stories crowding the front page of the newspapers, but what about those stories that were hidden in the small box on page one or in section B of the paper? The ones that didn't seem to draw the same attention. One of those was that of a twenty-three-year-old young woman who had gone missing. On the front page of the *Cincinnati Post* on December 19, 1997, a small story found on the right side of the page showed a small picture of Alana "Laney" Gwinner with her beautiful smile. At the time, Laney had been missing for nine days with no leads or ideas about where she or her car could be. Her friends and family had been searching every place they could possibly think Laney might go. Hundreds of phone calls to anyone that may have a connection with her had been made. There was still no sign of her.

I noticed that the article wasn't only about Laney. The article discussed other missing women, whom I later learned were considered deceased because of the time that had gone by since their disappearances. I felt a bit upset that the attention had been taken off Laney. I know that the author of that article was in no way trying to minimize Laney's story, and I'm not sure why it upset me like it did, other than the fact that her story had now seemed to become personal for Evan and me. Don't get me wrong, those other stories were extremely tragic in their own right and definitely deserved to have attention drawn to them. At the time, though, Laney was still out there, and finding her was at the top of the list for her family, friends, coworkers, and those who may have seen her that night.

December 9, 1997, was a normal day for Laney: get up early, prepare for work, and start the day like any other. According to her boss, she was a very conscientious, hard-working employee. Laney was always on time and ready to work. He said she would call before leaving home if she thought she was going to be late, even by one minute. This gained her great respect from her boss. These types of characteristics are often rewarded with a promotion, which is exactly what happened for Laney. Things were going well. Her life wasn't always easy, but for the moment, it appeared as if the stars were aligning for her, at least in her professional life.

Like most of us, distractions occur during the workday. Laney was no different. The morning of December 8th started out with a simple email to a friend, Angie, saying, *"What's up?"*

The work day continued, and Laney and Angie corresponded back and forth. Laney ended with telling Angie about having a confrontation with a female at her current boyfriend's house over the weekend. Angie responded about her day and asked more about the weekend events. Laney expressed her need to study for her accounting exam coming up the next day. She ended the conversation with, *"Give me a call later and I will fill you in on his reaction to the whole situation and try to get your input on it. I think Shad, Joy, and I are going to BW3's tomorrow after my exam, wanna go? Call me."*

It should be noted that in 1997, cell phones were not the extra appendage most people have today. If you had a cell phone, it was considered to be a luxury or it was specifically used for work.

That being said, the conversation ended at the end of the workday, and both went on with their separate lives that evening. Tuesday morning, December 9th, began with a continuation of the conversation from the day before.

Laney wrote, *"Nothing is up with Shad... He was out with Eric in Chicago all weekend. Eric said they had a blast, it was just like old times. We are just going to BW3's to chow down on some wings!!! Maybe shoot a little pool. Sound Good? I have my exam tonight so I don't know what time we are going."*

Unfortunately, Angie's son was sick, and she did not want to leave him with anyone, so she had to explain to Laney that she most likely would not make it that evening. That would be the last exchange Angie would have with her beloved friend.

Laney's day continued like normal. She knew that, at the end of the day, she would have to go take her exam. Like almost all students, she wasn't that excited to take that test. Did she study enough? Was she prepared, or was this going to turn out badly? Her boss remembered that she left a little early that day to put in a last few minutes studying before the exam.

Laney had made plans with friends to meet at BW3's near Forest Fair Mall later that evening to celebrate the end of classes.

The idea was to meet there to have some dinner and then venture somewhere to play some pool. Laney was an avid pool player. Some might even say she was a bit of a sandbagger. She would act like she didn't know how to play to lure someone, particularly a man, into a false sense of security, then proceed to kick their ass and take their money. This could be a good thing or it could be a bad thing, depending on who she was playing and how much she had taken from them. From stories I have heard about Laney, she wouldn't back down from anyone. She may have been small, but she was tough. Playing pool against her could start a ruckus.

During the day leading up to dinner, unfortunately, some of her friends contacted her to let her know that they would not be able to attend the get together. That left only Laney and her friend Shad to go out that evening. They arrived at Bdub's, as they called it, between eight and eight thirty p.m. They had a few drinks and downed those wings she liked so much. Between nine and nine thirty p.m., they arrived at the Gilmore Bowling Lanes in Fairfield, Ohio. It is not clear who decided to go there, because according to most people who knew her, she had never been to Gilmore Lanes until that night. How did they know that they could play pool there? Was it well known that Gilmore had pool tables? I guess we will never know the answer to that question, but that is where they ended up that night.

Gilmore Bowling Lanes has been in Fairfield for quite a long time. It actually used to go by the name of Coleman Lanes when I was a kid, but more than forty years later, it still looks almost exactly the same with only the name change. It's kind of funny how some places seem to get trapped in time. Like almost all bowling alleys, there are lanes in the back of the building, and out front there is a bar. Most of the bars I've seen in these alleys are not places you would take a date to dinner, but they do have alcohol, which draws all kinds of people. Most of those bars draw the bowlers in there in between frames, and then a few may stop in after bowling to have a nightcap before heading home.

This night seemed different for some reason.

The bar that night was a hopping place with a combination of bowlers, local car salesmen, pool players, and a group of friends partaking in a weeknight drinking party, just for the hell of it. This tiny bar was kind of crowded, especially for a Tuesday night. According to some of the workers, who still work there today, the bar usually closed around eleven thirty p.m. on a weeknight, but that night they stayed open because there were many people still having a good time and, well, that meant they were making a little extra cash. The question is why did everyone stay late that evening? Could it have been that beautiful, twenty-three-year-old woman with the jeans that fit just right and the brilliant smile that lit up a room? Laney was only one of two or possibly three women in that bar that night. There may have been an older woman who was a bit of a regular and an eighteen-year-old who was hiding in the corner drinking beer with her friends hoping that the cops didn't come in and catch her. The men were from different backgrounds and ages, and having a good time, but all must have noticed that beautiful girl playing pool. One person took a serious interest in the "hot girl" in the room.

As the night began to wind down, Laney had to go to the restroom, considering she'd had quite a few drinks while celebrating with Shad. Someone had stated they saw her stop by the payphone by the front door to make a call. It was later established that she did make a call to her current boyfriend to let him know, "I'm on my way." There may have been a few other calls made before she made it to the restroom, but she eventually made it there and returned to the bar to quickly say her goodbyes.

She slipped out the door without most people, including Shad, seeing her leave.

Somewhere between twelve thirty a.m. and one a.m., Alana "Laney" Gwinner, now trapped in time, slipped out into the dark, cold December night.

# 2

# May Pops

"Some things will always be mysteries. They can be explained, but they can't be understood."
— Erin Morgenstern, *The Night Circus*

DECEMBER 10, 1997, will haunt Laney's friends and family for the rest of their lives. For most, that Wednesday started as normal. Many had to get their kids ready for school, others had to get ready for work, but no one knew what was coming later that day. Rick, Laney's boss at Telco Communications, had a bad feeling when he got to work and Laney wasn't there. He worked his way around the office to find out if anyone had heard from Laney. Something was wrong. She was never late to work without calling, and that day she hadn't even shown up. Eight o'clock passed; nine o'clock went by. Where was she? Rick called her parents to see if she was sick. Did she get a late start? Was she taking the day off for some reason? It became very uncomfortable in the office. Anxiety was setting in because this was not the Laney that her boss knew.

When Rick called her parents, they seemed as if there was nothing to worry about. He didn't quite understand their reaction, but he also didn't know some of their family dynamics. Twenty-three-year-old Laney was known to spend the night at friends' houses any day of the week. She was also known to say she was going to one place and then on the way change her mind and end up somewhere else. Even her friends spoke of her frequently flying by the seat of her pants, whether it was to go to a boyfriend's house or to head home. Laney was like a feather in the wind, landing somewhere lightly after the breeze died down.

As the day wore on, the strange feeling started to spread to many people. Her current boyfriend, of only six weeks or so, woke up early in the morning before his work with a landscaping company to find that Laney wasn't there. Concerned, he called a friend of Laney's to ask, "Hey, have you heard from Laney? Did she come to stay with you last night?" Not able to get hold of the friend, he left a voicemail in hopes that she would get the message soon.

That afternoon, phones frantically rang and pager buzzes filled the silence as friends communicated their concerns for Laney's whereabouts. "Hey, have you seen Laney?" "When was the last time you talked to Laney?" "Did you see Laney last night or this morning? She isn't at work." With each call, the fear rose. Where was Alana "Laney" Gwinner? The number of individuals searching for her grew with each passing hour. At around noon, all of her friends, especially Angie, started to think the worst had happened to Laney. Laney had missed lunch with Angie, which was unusual in itself, but this day was especially significant because it was Angie's birthday. Laney had had lunch with her on her birthday for several years now, and Laney would never miss that important day.

Soon, groups of friends got together to start a search for Laney. They met at the bowling alley where Laney had last been seen and brainstormed all the places to look, every phone number to call, and all the possible scenarios of where Laney could be. They broke up into small search parties, going to some of their usual hangouts, such as the Cheyenne Cattle Company bar and nightclub at Forest Fair Mall. Laney's friends had spent a great deal of time dancing, drinking, and having fun at this club. Did Laney go there after leaving the bowling alley? Did anyone there see her or see her leave with anyone? Did she possibly go see a former boyfriend? Did she go to a friend's house that wasn't checked yet? Did she have an accident? Where was her car? All of these questions would eventually disappear into the darkness as time went by, hour by hour, day by day, week by week. How did Laney simply vanish?

After all the places had been searched and people close to her had been contacted, Laney's friends went to her family, who had been doing some searching on their own, to convince them that the police needed to be called. By then, Alana had been gone for two full days, and her parents decided it was time to tell the police that something seemed really wrong.

The Liberty Township, Ohio, Police Department took the initial report. They told the family they would look into it, but then they realized the incident in question had occurred in Fairfield, Ohio. On Saturday, December 13th, Liberty Township police sent over the initial report to the Fairfield Police Department. Laney had now been gone for three full days. So much could happen in three days. Was Laney hurt somewhere and stuck out in the cold? Did someone take her, and if so, what were they doing with her? Unfortunately, those awful thoughts started to creep into the minds of every person close to her.

Laney's story had now hit the newspapers and TV newscasts across the city. Interest in her whereabouts started to build. Most of us watching the news see a story like this, feel sorry for the family, and hope she will be found in good health as soon as possible, but it's news that really doesn't affect us. To her family, friends, class-mates, and people at that bar, it hit pretty hard. *Wow! Someone we know or have seen is missing.* Missing is a term that can be both posi-tive and negative at the same time. Missing means she may still be out there and she will come home soon; missing can also mean something bad has happened.

On Monday, December 15, 1997, the Fairfield police were now five days behind in their search for the missing girl from the bowling alley. The first step was to go to the bowling alley to take a look at the last place she was known to be. During the day, the bowling alley looks completely different than it does at night. During the day, the busy intersection right in front of the alley is packed with cars and hundreds of possible witnesses. The alley itself is a ghost town at this time because of the natural progression of the day. Most people who frequent the bowling alley have jobs during the afternoon hours. The only people there are the workers preparing for the busy night that will follow as the work whistles blow at the end of the day.

The investigators started with the workers and owners to find out the ins and outs of the bowling alley. What was the schedule of leagues? Who tended bar? What were the hours of operation? Were there cameras in the parking lot? All the basic information about the area she was last seen. Unfortunately, the answers to these ques-tions didn't have an immediate connection to what went on at the bowling alley at night. The investigators had to return after dark to see what it was like. They had to question everyone that may have been there during the weeknights, especially on Tuesdays.

They continued to talk with friends, family, ex-boyfriends, current boyfriend, and others to gain knowledge of Laney's normal movements. Time was of the essence, but time was slipping away.

Anyone who has general knowledge of investigations knows that the first forty-eight hours are the most crucial times to gain leads, but this investigation really didn't get started until 120 hours later. Time became the enemy. It was moving so fast yet so slow.

One week became two. Two weeks became three, and hope started to fade into the darkness of the cold, short days of winter. Loved ones held on to hope because that's all they had. Perhaps this was merely a dream and Laney would walk through that door at any time. Sadly, that did not happen. Each day passed without that beautiful young woman. She was apparently lost to the demons of that fateful night. As we know, life goes on. Even though some people spent much of their time looking for Laney, they also had to keep up their regular lives, going to work and taking care of their families. The search gradually started to wane as the inevitable seemed to become a reality. Alana "Laney" Gwinner was gone, vanished into the shadows of that cold December morning.

Christmas and New Year's had come and gone with a huge hole in the hearts of many close to Laney. The new year would also bring more heartache to the Cincinnati area. On January 4, 1998, exactly one month after losing Officers Daniel Pope and Ronald Jeter, during a pursuit of a possible drunk driver, Officer Michael Partin parked his car to join the foot pursuit of the suspect driver. The chase occurred on the Clay Wade Bailey Bridge spanning the Ohio River from Covington, Kentucky, to Cincinnati, Ohio. This bridge has a section for cars that is adjacent to a section that allows people to walk along that bridge. The suspect and the pursuing officer had jumped from the road to the walking section of the bridge. Officer Partin was attempting to cut off the suspect when he missed the walkway railing. He slipped through, falling approximately ninety feet into the river below. Officer Partin disappeared into the dark, cold Ohio River and did not resurface. It would take months to find him.

The search for Officer Partin started almost immediately. Dive teams, police boats, and water rescue teams all quickly arrived at the scene. Unfortunately, darkness had already set in, so the search would be very difficult. The police chief deemed the rescue operation too dangerous to continue. He told the teams to stop for the night. The search for Officer Partin's body would reconvene at daylight.

The Ohio Valley area was having a rough year with rain that affected the swift currents of the Ohio River. The river was moving about three and a half to four miles per hour to the southwest. Search crews would try to take this into consideration when looking for Officer Partin, creating a search area and using sonar to try to locate him. The dark, murky water made finding his body extremely difficult and dangerous. The search continued for the next several days in hopes of possibly getting lucky enough to find Partin's remains.

On January 7th, Mother Nature paid the greater Cincinnati area another visit with a strong dose of rain, delaying the search for multiple days. When the search continued, the river was racing at approximately four and a half miles per hour. Many may think this doesn't seem very fast, but if you have ever witnessed a swollen river after rain, you would understand that four and a half miles per hour is extremely fast. The power of water at those speeds can be treacherous to anything that stands in its way. The river was mad, and a small boat used by dive teams could have some serious trouble. The local police departments decided a helicopter would be the safest way to search for Officer Partin.

On January 10, 1998, the helicopter took off from Lunken Airport on the southeast side of Cincinnati. The pilot maneuvered the craft up and down the winding river as if following the backbone of a serpent, checking from the center of the river to the bank in hopes that something of Michael's could be seen. The search that day brought no solace to Michael's family, friends, and fellow police officers, as there was no sign of him. The light of winter dwindled early, putting a stop to that day's search for Officer Michael Partin.

Determined not to give up, the pilot, along with the Covington fire chief, resumed the hunt for Michael around ten a.m. on Sunday, January 11, 1998. The flight took off from the same airport in Cincinnati, following the same route as the previous day. The view in the wintertime gives the vision of an Ansel Adams black-and-white picture. The foliage on the trees had been gone for a while, and the dark river water contrasted against the lighter-colored lines of the shore. The river seemed angry after the large rainfall of January 7th, with its fast-moving waters carrying large trees as if they were toothpicks. Finding a body was going to be difficult, but they pushed on down the river in search of the fallen officer.

As the helicopter made it to the bend in the Ohio River near the mouth of the Big Sugar Creek, Captain Reinhart of the Covington Fire Department spotted some color in the black-and-white backdrop. There seemed to be shades of blue and off-white in the middle of the river known as the dead zone. Even though this term seemed appropriate for the discovery to come, it actually refers to the area in the river where the current rotates in a circle to slow down objects floating in the center of the river. As the pilot maneuvered closer, they saw a body. Captain Reinhart could immediately tell it was a female by the shape of the body, along with the blue jeans and blue-and-white striped sweater that appeared to be pushed up toward her head.

In reality, finding a body floating in the dead zone was actually very surprising to the helicopter pilot and Captain Reinhart. The two of them had followed the river most of the day on January 10th, searching for the police officer. The actual idea they would find him was truly wishful thinking, but they did it anyway because you never give up on a search for a fallen officer. The reason it was wishful thinking was the river water was well below 50° F and, from experience, Captain Reinhart knew that cold water tended to preserve a body at the bottom of the river. This is where the science of decomposition and water retrieval overlap.

Many readers of this book likely have heard of the "Body Farm" at the University of Tennessee's Anthropological Research Facility. The research done there is groundbreaking regarding the decomposition of human remains under different conditions. Most research is done on bodies placed in mostly terrestrial environments. The research facilitators usually look at the progression of insects, especially flies, on the body to determine how long it takes for it to become completely skeletonized. The studies have gleaned a huge amount of data to help forensic scientists determine how long a body has been exposed to the specific environment in which it is found. Scientists have determined that decomposition progresses rapidly in warmer temperatures, while cooler temperatures tend to slow it down.

During my research into decomposition in water, I have found there is really not much data available. So I went out to find an expert on this topic. With some help from Mark Reiber, a retired police detective, we found someone who has spent many years retrieving individuals from the water. In most cases, Ken Purcell, from the Boone County Water Rescue Team, retrieves living people, but unfortunately in this line of business, there are those horrific days of finding bodies in the water. Ken enlightened us on decomposition in water.

Water is an intriguing chemical compound on its own. Water can do so many things, and we all know it is what keeps the human body alive. Water is also extremely powerful in many ways. One characteristic of water is that it takes enormous energy and time to raise its temperature, but it also holds on to that temperature for a very long time. Mr. Purcell explained to me that as the fall season approaches the Midwest, the ambient temperature begins to fall. The water from the Ohio River and surrounding tributaries are still a bit warmer than the ambient temperature. We could go through all the properties of energy transfer, but to most, this may be a little boring, so I'm simply going to say that the heat from the water collides with the slower molecules in the cooler air, causing the water temperature to begin to fall. This continues as winter starts to creep in. Eventually, the river water drops down to very cold temperatures, and it will take a very long time to bring them back up in the spring and summer months in the Ohio Valley area. November through March in Cincinnati usually gets very cold, and the river temperatures are well below 40° F. The river water acts like a refrigerator on bodies that fall into them during these time periods. That means that it is going to take a very long time to reach the point, approximately 50° F, in which the body will decompose enough to bloat and float up to the surface.

Mr. Purcell continued to tell me the bodies that go into the water in the winter most likely will not surface until May, if they ever surface at all. In the months of May and June, more bodies are found than in any other month because the water temperatures are warm enough to cause the bacteria in the internal organs to start to decompose the body. In that process, the by-product of decomposition is gas, which will eventually increase the buoyancy of the body and cause it to float to the top of the water. In the gallows humor of those who deal with death on a daily basis, Mr. Purcell said he and his colleagues term these bodies as "May Pops."

January 11, 1998, is the day that anyone who knew Laney Gwinner would mourn for the rest of their lives. That female body found in blue jeans and a sweater floating in the dead zone of the Ohio River was Laney. Thirty-one days after she was last seen alive, her somewhat well-preserved body was found face down on the top of the water nearly fifty miles from where she had last been seen. How did she get so far from home? How did she get into the river? Did she accidentally drive into it after leaving the bowling alley? Was there something her friends didn't know about her that she may have done this to herself? Did someone do this to her, and if so, what else did they do to her? These are the questions that started running through everyone's minds when she was found. The biggest question of them all was WHY? Why did the life of such a beautiful young lady end way too soon? If it wasn't an accident or suicide, why would anyone want to hurt her? Why? Why? Why? These were the same questions being asked by those who would begin the investigation into her death.

For Captain Reinhart and later Ken Purcell, there was another mystery. Why was she floating on the surface of the river in the middle of January? If she had gone into the water in December, her body should have gone to the bottom of the river as her lungs filled up with water. The river was cold, so how did she start decomposition to the point she was bloated and on top of the river so soon? It was almost as if Officer Partin was underneath the water, pushing her to the surface to be found. If science and experience were correct, Laney Gwinner should have been a "May Pop."

# 3

# The Car

"**Missing pieces do more than complete the puzzle, they fill in an empty space.**"
— Luanne Rice

A BODY HAD BEEN FOUND in the murky water of the Ohio River. At the time of the recovery, a barge was making its way up the river toward Cincinnati. The local sheriff had been contacted about the spotting of the body from the air, and he was able to radio the barge workers to ask for their help in securing the body until the water rescue team could arrive. The sheriff and his crew manned a boat to complete the recovery.

Once on the shore, the investigation into who this poor young woman was started with something simple: a search through the pockets of her jeans. In the back pocket was a driver's license and about six dollars. The driver's license was that of Alana J. Gwinner from Cincinnati, Ohio. It seemed fitting that during the search for a man who dedicated his life to protecting and serving others, the body of a young girl who was taken in the dark was found. It's almost as if Officer Michael Partin led that helicopter down the river to find her.

At last, Laney's family and friends at least knew where she was.

At last, Laney was no longer missing.

Even though the process of the investigation had just begun, immediate questions were formed.

Who was Alana J. Gwinner, and why was she in the Ohio River?

Where did she enter the river?

When did she enter the river?

The most important question was: HOW did she enter the river?

There was a great deal of work to be done after her recovery. The first step was to get her to the morgue, contact the Fairfield, Ohio, Police Department, and schedule an autopsy. The autopsy is a necessary evil of death investigation. As most readers of true crime stories know, the autopsy should expose the cause of death. The coroner would determine the cause as well as the manner of death. The cause may actually not be as important as the manner. The cause of death could have been any number of things, but the manner of death—accident, suicide, homicide, or natural—determines the next steps in the case.

In Laney's case, the coroner said the cause of death was asphyxiation prior to entering the water. Although the coroner had reservations at first, he went on to state the manner of death to be the worst conclusion imaginable: homicide.

Homicide. We hear this term all the time on TV, in podcasts, and read it in print, but to most of us, it's just a word to describe a horrible act. It has a sorrowful connotation, but unless you have lived it through a family member or friend, it's merely a descriptive word. Losing a loved one has occurred in almost everyone's life, but for most of us, it was because of an accident, a health issue, or it was simply that person's time to join their maker. Those losses, of course, are tragic, but at least in those situations the cause and manner of death have answers. The "why" and "how" can feel cloudy and hard to accept, but you can at least see through the tears to somewhat understand them.

Homicide is different. It's cold and lonely and impossible to understand. I did not realize its gravity until I looked at Laney's autopsy. Although I personally did not know her, I felt as if I did in a way by looking through that document given to me by her brother. As I sifted through Laney's case file, I stumbled upon some black and white pictures I wish I had never seen. In deep contrast to the happy, bright pictures I had seen of her with her friends on earlier carefree nights out on the town, the images of her body in that state after the autopsy are ones I wish I could erase from my memory, yet I need to remember them to stay focused on telling her story. If you are a believer in some sort of life after death, then picture Laney as a beautiful winged angel looking over her family and friends in the absence of her earthly body. Her physical body, however, tells the story of that fateful night in hopes that it will help those still here on Earth find the monster that took her from here way too early.

Homicide is defined as one human being causing the death of another. The term seems so direct, yet if you have any feelings about the word, it makes you cringe. The term takes on a whole different meaning as you think about the events of that night. Your imagination runs wild, especially if you knew her or you have looked into this case so much that you feel like you knew her, as I do. Murder in this sense means that Laney most likely put up a fight. The suspect had to physically subdue her enough to hold her for several minutes to cause her to stop breathing. What did she go through before she was put into that cold river? Who could do this to someone so young with a full life ahead of her? Did they mean to do it or was it an accident and they panicked?

Endless questions still yet to be answered.

The investigation now took on a new sense of urgency. While Laney was missing, the investigation zeroed in on this question: What are all the possible places she could have gone after leaving that bowling alley? She was known to have called her boyfriend to tell him she was on her way over, but he stated she never made it. She had a previous boyfriend whom she called the love of her life who was supposedly out of town, but she was known to run off to see him randomly at any time. There was an abusive ex-boyfriend that she argued with a few weeks before her disappearance. Her free spirit left the possibilities wide open. But once her body was found in the river, the search for details of that night had to shift to thinking about those who could or would hurt her.

The big problem was the fact that Laney had been found in the river. As we said before, water brought on a whole different set of issues. Evidence can be washed away, especially in the fast moving, rain-swollen waters of the Ohio River. Trace evidence like hair and fibers, unless embedded into the clothes or her hair, could have easily been swept away. Even though DNA technology was advancing in the 1990s, it still had a long way to go. The methods of extraction from a victim's clothing, skin, or hair were limited and might not find DNA as compared to the methods now available. Plus, DNA exposed to the elements can easily break down before the police could collect it.

So what usable evidence did the police have left?

Well, let's talk about the different types of evidence often found at a crime scene or on a victim. The true crime craze probably started in October of 2000, when the popular TV show *CSI* first hit television screens. The intriguing characters, cool science stuff, and the fact the suspect was always captured at the end of a sixty-minute program drew people in hook, line, and sinker. I'll admit I was one of those who loved the show. The problem with the show was it created a false narrative that all police departments will be able to find evidence that will directly lead to the killer and will be able to do so quickly and neatly.

Even though the crime shows use some real terms and occasionally follow some procedures that real detectives might use, the true story is that a real-world murder case does not work that easily. According to the FBI's Criminal Justice Information Services (CJIS), since 1960, there are more than 250,000 families in the United States who don't have answers, with the numbers climbing each year. In the state of Ohio, the Ohio Attorney General's page documents 2,310 unsolved murders, and that does not include Laney's case. The numbers could be much more than what has been reported because not all cases are reported to those keeping track of these astonishing numbers.

In almost all of those cases, the reason they are unsolved is the lack of evidence. What is frustrating is the fact that oftentimes police have a serious person of interest in the case, and all it would take is one piece of evidence to tie them to the scene. That crucial piece of evidence is not there, or if it is, it hasn't been found yet.

There are many different types of evidence. There are those pieces of evidence that are considered *class* evidence. This is evidence that can be shared by a large number of people. For example, finding a brown hair on a victim's clothing doesn't really tell us much. There are nearly eight billion people in the world, and some studies say that 90 percent of the world's population has brown or black hair. Those certainly aren't very good numbers when trying to narrow down the suspect pool.

*Trace* evidence often falls under the category of class evidence. Trace evidence is evidence that oftentimes is difficult to see with the naked eye and can easily be missed in a crime scene situation. Animal hair, dirt particles, or fibers from a shirt or blanket can be considered trace evidence.

*Circumstantial* evidence is evidence that may not directly connect someone to a crime, but due to the type of evidence, the amount of evidence, and the connection to a person, it may give the detectives the ability to make inferences on the strength of that connection. In my class, I try to give the students a simple example of this in a scenario:

*You are having a party at your house and some of your friends are inside the house while you are with other friends outside. Suddenly, you hear loud noises and things breaking inside the house. You rush inside to see one of your friends laying on the floor with a bloody nose, next to a broken coffee table, with another friend standing over them. The evidence is the noises you heard, the broken table, the bloody nose, and the one person standing over the other. Some people seem to be upset with the situation, so you begin to make inferences about what must have occurred. The circumstance appears to be that a fight had broken out and the person standing must have inflicted a wound on the person on the floor.*

The question I always ask my students is: Did you see it happen? The answer is always, "No, but..." Well, that is my simple version of circumstantial evidence. Did we see it? "No, but..." with all the pieces put together, the actions we described are the most logical in the situation.

Then there is *individual* evidence. This is exactly what it sounds like. This is evidence that will lead directly to an individual who possibly could have been the perpetrator. The perfect individual evidence we all know is DNA. DNA technology has made huge strides since 1986 when it was first used to solve a case. The procedures to extract DNA from almost anything have changed forensic science and crime solving, especially in the last five years. Every day in the news we see stories of murders being solved thirty, forty, fifty, and even sixty years after the crime had occurred. If these murders can be solved, why can't they all? Why is the murder of Alana "Laney" Gwinner still unsolved after twenty-five years?

The evidence doesn't seem to be there.

I could go into the evidence that I know about, but I'm not going to do that. One of the statements that was given to us by police departments and prosecutors is, "According to Ohio Ordinance 149.43 this is still an open case, therefore evidentiary information will not be released." After receiving this statement over and over again, it can get frustrating. The fact that there could be some information or evidence that cannot be disclosed to those seeking to help is beyond disappointing. It hurts to know that potentially in that vault of evidence there may lie a clue that will allow Laney's family to find some glimmer of peace. However, I also understand why they do this. I don't want to give out the information that was found for the same reason: It may be key to solving the case one day.

With nothing to go on, what does a police department do? They had to try interviewing as many people as possible who may have seen or heard anything related to Laney's disappearance and death. All leads called in have be followed until they cannot be followed any further. Talking with anyone who may have been there that night that may have seen something they did not know was important was crucial. The detectives had to speak with friends, family, coworkers, enemies, boyfriends, classmates, and anyone who may have known Laney in any special way to see if anything would give insight into who she was and what may have changed that night to put her in danger. This is known as victimology, and we will discuss this in more detail later in the book, but it was something Fairfield detectives had to do to find that needle in the haystack.

Through conversations, the police were able to determine a few things about Laney that could have been of importance. Things like a fight with an ex-boyfriend. The confrontation with a female the week before, a current boyfriend who lived close, and the love of her life who did not live close might have been important. It came to light that there were individuals in that bar that night fighting their own demons with violent tendencies. Unfortunately, none of the information gathered garnered any evidence usable for the case. Did it create persons of interest? Yes. As a matter of fact, there were many of them, which created a whole lot of problems. From the conversations, there was one thing that was missing from the bowling alley that could have held the evidence needed to capture the individual responsible for Laney's death. Laney and Shad, her friend, had met at BW3's prior to going to Gilmore Lanes. If they met there, then they both had to have driven there or been dropped off. According to Shad, they met to eat and then proceeded to drive separately to the bowling alley. So where was Laney's car?

One of the things Laney was so proud of, according to family and friends, was the purchase of her 1993 Honda Del Sol. A beautiful black sports car with a red interior, it was a car that fit her personality—sleek and fun. The search by friends and family for Laney in the days right after her disappearance began by going to the last place she had been seen, but one thing that wasn't there was *the car*. The individuals searching were convinced that if they found the car, they would find Laney. The assumption was that the car had to be the key to her whereabouts. Once the police were involved and it appeared to be a dire situation, an APB was put out on the 1993 black Honda Del Sol, Ohio License Plate AKP-3607.

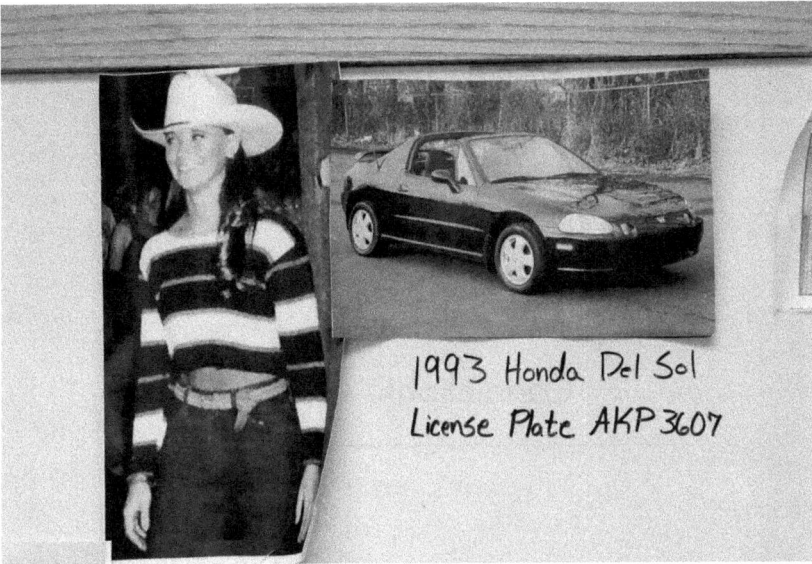

1993 Honda Del Sol
License Plate AKP 3607

It was nearly a week after her disappearance before that APB was put out. A week for Lancy to drive a long way if she was trying to escape from the world she lived in. It also was a week for someone to do something with Laney and get rid of the car. Calls flooded in from all over the city of sightings of a black Honda Del Sol, but none resulted in finding the correct vehicle. By then, it appeared that Laney had been lured into the darkness and was likely dead. It seemed that the right evidence to solve this case, the car, was going to be really difficult to find, and time became the enemy.

Where was the car?

# 4

# Candlelight's Gleam

*The call came, the one that I have dreaded*
*Telling me the worst, your life had truly ended*
*I still had hope, that you'd come home safe and sound*
*It didn't happen that way, but finally, you were found*
*The days since you've been gone have gone by in a blur*
*How I'm making it by, I'm really not too sure*
*I keep my mind moving, never letting myself think*
*For fear, I might break down, for fear my heart*
    *would sink*
*I see your face on the news and your name echoes in*
    *my ear*
*I have to keep busy, I'm so afraid of my tears*
*My tears are the reminder that you are gone, you're*
    *really gone*
*I tell myself it wasn't you, it can't be you, I have to be*
    *strong*
*I'm remembering though all those years we spent*
    *together*

*So many memories, I can't forget, not now, not ever*
*As the call comes flooding back, I have to stop and*
    *catch my breath*
*We thought we knew it all, nothing could touch us, not*
    *even death*
*But reality sets in, my body grows numb*
*My heart is breaking, and that won't change no matter*
    *how far I run*
*I miss you so much, the pain is too much to bear*
*Your face, your voice, your smile to which no one can*
    *compare*
*Your life has touched us all from beginning to end*
*Each at different stages only time can mend*
*Each of us love you for the beautiful person you are*
    *inside*
*And now that you are gone, a part of us too has died*
*We come together to remember how special you*
    *truly are*
*Knowing that you're shining, for you are that brightest*
    *star*
*Your spirit lives in each one of our hearts*
*Echoing "Friends Forever," together or apart*
*Our love burns eternal in a candlelight's gleam*
*So, for now Laney, sleep tight and sweet dreams*

– Stacy (MaClanahan) Ross
Friend of Laney's

FIVE YEARS AGO, a bright young man in my class, Evan Fletcher, and I set out to challenge ourselves by diving into the research of cold cases. Like most people, mysteries intrigued us, and with the recent enthusiasm placed on web sleuths and true crime, we jumped right in. We had come across documentaries like the *Smiley Face Killers* and *The Disappearance of Crystal Rogers*. The interesting details and the bizarre happenings in those cases drew us into the strings connecting the components of the investigative process.

We had to narrow down which of the overwhelming number of cold cases to explore. Evan would email or text me during the school day, "What about this one?" I would respond with, "Looks good, but what about this one?" Needless to say, both his schoolwork and mine—shhh, don't tell my principal—were slightly interrupted for a period of time. Then for some reason, nearly at the exact same moment, we both sent each other a link to a Facebook page, "Who Killed Missy Witt?" This Facebook page is dedicated to telling the story of Melissa Witt, from Fort Smith, Arkansas, and the search for her killer. The reason we both connected with this page was that, on or near the day we were researching cold cases, the author of the page, LaDonna Humphrey, who I will talk about later, had posted a set of details that seemed to have linked Missy's case to a case right up the road from us in Fairfield. It was a description of similarities between Missy's disappearance and that of Laney's. Evan and I thought it was weird we both hit that page at about the same time, and we both thought Laney's was a good story to look into since it was so close to us. I also had kind of a personal connection to the story since I was a Fairfield native, and growing up, it always seemed to be a cozy, blue-collar, nothing-ever-happens-here town.

We started by reading that Facebook page, then found news articles on Newspapers.com, and even realized that the local FOX19 News had recently aired a story on Laney in a segment called "Crime Vault," narrated and produced by local reporter

Jessica Schmidt. Jessica and LaDonna would soon become very important to our work; we just didn't know it at that time.

Our document dig and data collection would continue for hours at a time. Evan and I would stay after school until seven, eight, and even nine p.m. working on what to do next and who to contact. I will go deeper into this work later in the book, but as we were doing all of this, I began to realize we hadn't gotten to know Laney except for what was printed on paper or spoken in news reports or podcasts. I began to feel a little guilty because I can honestly say I had never heard her story until that day in 2018. I couldn't understand how I had missed this awful story of her death. I guess the only way to explain it was that it wasn't personal to me. We all live in our own bubble, only acknowledging the things that affect us the most. Laney wasn't my relative or my friend. If I even paid attention to the news, I'm sure I was heartbroken for the family and mad that someone could do this, but my life revolved around my family and myself.

If I did read the paper—which sounds bad for a teacher—or watched the news, I spent most of my time looking at the local sports stories or results. At the time, I was a football, wrestling, and track coach, and sports had always been a major part of my life. A sad story of a young woman gone missing and later found dead was terrible to hear, but like I said, it wasn't close to me. So why all of a sudden did I find myself spending an enormous amount of time trying to find out who she was and what happened to her? Was it only my curiosity or was there some type of divine intervention? Was it meant to be that Evan would strike up that conversation with me about cold cases? Was Laney reaching out to me to say, "Hey, now it is time to get to know me?" What was it? I'm not sure if I believe in coincidences or fate, but something weird was happening, and it would not let go.

The progress continued, but then I told Evan we had to do

more. We had to get to know who Laney was. I don't know if it was because my daughter was twenty-three, and that was the age Laney was when she ran into that monster, or if looking at her pictures reminded me that Laney was much more than what happened to her, but I knew we had to start talking to those closest to her.

LaDonna, in her book *The Girl I Never Knew*, described words used in articles like "beautiful female murder victim" or "attractive" as terms that superficially described the victim. As I look at my floor covered with newspaper articles, photos, yearbooks, memorials, and cards to her parents, I realize those same terms could be found in Laney's stories. Some at first glance seem like mere words on a page, but then the more connected I became to Laney, the more those words began to sting. I can't imagine how Laney's mother and father felt as they read those articles. One headline read "Missing Woman," while another called her a "Union Township Woman." She has a name! It's Alana, or Laney, for God's sake, so call her by her name.

The rain we had experienced in January of that year continued through the spring. This sparked an article printed on April 20, 1998, titled "River yields debris, bodies." I understand what the writer was trying to portray, but to call the humans found in the river that year "debris" I find a bit offensive. The one that hurt me the most was in an article published by the *Cincinnati Post* on Monday, January 13, 1998, two days after Laney was found in the river. The story described how Laney was found in the middle of the river, and the reporter quoted what the Kentucky state police officer said about that discovery. Now, I know that the officer had no idea who the young woman was who was floating in the river, and I'm sure he had seen his share of deceased individuals, but when talking to the reporter, he referred to Laney's body as "*it.*" "*It* was in the middle of the river." "I know *it* wasn't put in the river in our area." This didn't sit well with me at all. At point, I knew the biggest part of looking into Laney's case was to find out exactly who Laney was.

So the search began. Who were Laney's friends? Were there any family members we could possibly contact? Would childhood friends still be able to describe what she was like? Were friends still focused on what happened to her, or had they tried to move on because the pain was too crippling? Evan was a master at finding information. I would throw an idea at him about what information we needed to find, and within minutes, he would respond, "Got it."

That night after our conversation about finding those close to her, Evan and I had stayed up late to determine which people we knew we had to speak with. Of course, Evan is a lot younger than me, so I would say he probably stayed up much later than I did. When we arrived at school the next morning, he had a list of names and a message he had sent to all of them that night. I thought to myself, *Wow, this kid is good.* He also told me that we had a phone conversation with one of her friends scheduled for after school that day. I said, "Well, okay, here we go."

That day set off a firestorm of information that would continue for the next two years. That information flow would eventually slow down a bit because many people did not want to talk anymore or some didn't respond to us. But for now, we were getting somewhere, and the first thing we wanted to know from those that knew her was who she was.

What would I see if I met her for the first time?

If I had been with her and her friends back then, what would I find in her?

In most of the pictures I see of her, she seems to be happy. Was she always happy or was there another side to her?

We had so many more questions to ask, but now we were beginning to get the true sense of the real person behind that beautiful smile.

"She was so kind," said one friend.

"She would do anything for anyone," said another.

"She had dreams of getting married and having kids," was heard in many of our conversations.

Alana "Laney" Gwinner, twenty-three years old, 5'2" tall, 120 pounds. She had long brunette hair that stood out when she wore the white cowboy hat she loved so much. She had a beautiful smile and personality that would light up a room, according to those who knew her. She was kind but scrappy. Laney would be willing to give her time to lend an ear to someone who needed comfort or needed to blow off some steam. As we looked at her pictures in those country-western outfits, we could almost feel the fun she and her friends would have at the bars, especially at the Cheyenne Cattle Company.

The local country bar was fairly new at the time, but it became all the craze, because it was a place for young people in the area to go and show off their line-dancing skills to classic 1990s country music. Evan is too young for that music, but for me, I could hear Alan Jackson's "Chattahoochee," Toby Keith's "Should Have Been a Cowboy," or Shania Twain's "Any Man of Mine," the women's anthem of the time, echoing through a large building, along with the stomping of the boots and the screams of "Yee Haw!" Places like that were our generation's social media. If you were looking to find someone to hang out with for the night—or for some, their possible forever—these were the types of places you would go. For those of us, like my wife and me, we already had our forever, but we would go to those bars to have fun with our groups of friends and to "people watch" everyone who was trying to impress someone.

Laney, obviously, would catch the attention of many in a place like that, from the desperate fella who would annoyingly approach her several times during that fateful night only to get rejected, to the couples who saw humor in watching that guy try so hard. From what I have heard from her friends, a place like Cheyenne's was Laney's element. She was confident, fun, and loved celebrating life at those moments.

Like most young people between the ages of twenty-one and twenty-five, Laney was searching for her place in life. The teenage years of no responsibilities and just having fun were over, and adulthood was staring her right in the face. What did that mean, though? Those of us who have passed through that time period of our lives remember those days as filled with both excitement and fear. The exhilarating prospect of starting a new career or life with a significant other was hard to describe. Every day the butterflies in the stomach would flutter around because of the need to feel productive in your job or career choice. Also, there was the constant fear of failure or missing out on something or someone. Laney was twenty-three, that age right in the middle of the transition in which major life decisions seemed to be the only things facing a person. Back in the 1980s and '90s, we still had the family traditions that a young person felt they had to live up to in order to feel successful. A job by twenty-one or twenty-two years of age, to show you are growing up. Moved out on your own by twenty-three or twenty-four. And married with children on the way by twenty-six or twenty-seven. We know that doesn't work out for everyone, nor should it, but there was a pressure to fit the norms.

Laney was fulfilling one of those goals by completing her degree and working her way up in her job. The characteristic of hard work had been instilled in her by her father, and she was not going to disappoint him. Financial independence was something we all strived for in our twenties, because then it meant we didn't have to answer to Mom and Dad anymore, but sometimes that took longer than expected. Laney was working on that, but having fun was still of major importance, which I'm pretty sure was one of the priorities we all had for as long as we possibly could.

One thing that everyone I spoke to about Laney mentioned was her overwhelming selflessness. She was known to lend a hand wherever was needed, including being a surrogate big sister for a young girl who longed for a role model. As I have navigated this process of finding out who Laney truly was, her friend Brittany gave me the name of one of Laney's bosses at the job she had when her beautiful story took a tragic turn.

Shortly after I contacted this individual, I received a message that read, "Thank you for contacting me, but I think my daughter would be a better person to talk to about Laney. She spent many hours every day with her in our office while I had to work." I quickly texted back, "That would be awesome! Thank you very much." He forwarded a phone number to me, no name. I had no idea who I was contacting, but I didn't care. I was so excited to get the opportunity to speak with someone who spent almost every day with Laney. Who else would be able to tell me Laney's true character than someone who was with her that often? I wanted to give the young woman a chance to understand what I was doing before I cold-called her, so I sent a reaffirming message: "I know this is a rough topic, but your father told me you would be a great person to talk to about who Laney Gwinner was as a person. I hope you give it some thought and when you are ready please give me a call. If you do not feel comfortable speaking with me, I completely understand." Then I patiently waited for a response. Within a few days, my phone rang, and I hurried to answer it.

"Hello."

A calm voice said, "Hello, Mr. Hubbard."

"Yes," I responded.

"This is Aby Overbay. Do you remember me?" she said.

For a second, I was a bit perplexed. Then she said, "I was in your Forensic Science class back in 2005 at Mason."

"Oh, yes, the shot-putter! I had no idea you were the one I would be talking to."

This was only one of the strange connections to Laney I had experienced throughout this process. I will discuss many of these weird links to Laney's story at the end of the book, but each one made me more convinced that Laney was reaching out to me. She wanted me to know I was doing the right thing and that these were not coincidences. These were signs telling me to keep going because there was more to come.

Speaking with a former student who struggled a bit through school but is now a mother and doing well warms my heart, especially when they remember you and actually remember something you taught them almost twenty years ago. But I never would have thought I would be talking to a former student about a twenty-three-year-old girl who went missing in 1997 and was later found dead in the Ohio River.

When she was in my class, we worked on things like blood spatter, entomology, and fingerprints. We talked about the famous cases that almost everyone knew, but we never talked about cases like Laney's. As a matter of fact, I had not even heard about Laney's case up to that point, so it seemed really strange that I was talking to Aby twenty years later about Laney.

When I asked Aby to describe her relationship with Laney, she started off really quiet. If you would have known Aby as a teenager, quiet probably wasn't a word you would have used to describe her, so I knew talking about Laney was difficult for her. Aby was emotional about Laney's role in her life. At the age of ten and being an only child, Aby didn't have many people to look up to other than her parents. Laney filled that empty space for Aby. She was "like a big sister" she never had. In a world where both parents work, sometimes children have to go to work with their parents after school, on snow days, or when school is out of session, and

Aby was one of those kids. She would be picked up from school every day by her father, who would take her to work with him.

As Aby entered the door of her dad's company, Laney would be there with a warm smile and a snack for her. In between taking calls at the front desk or accomplishing tasks given to Laney by her boss, Laney would go into a conference room to help Aby with her homework or just to sit and talk. Aby didn't want to refer to Laney as a high-priced babysitter, but it kind of turned out that way. She would make sure that Aby was fed, she would make sure Aby was finishing her homework, and most of all, she would make sure Aby knew everything about makeup and how to use it. Laney was the one to always brighten Aby's day.

Whether it was an impressionable ten-year-old looking for that female idol to look up to, or a group of rowdy friends on a Friday night, Laney was the light to brighten the room. She was there for her friends in their times of need and there for the young girl who maybe had a bad day at school. Laney was finding her way in life, from finishing up classes at college or trying to find Mr. Right in a crowd of Mr. Wrongs. She could show the calming compassion a friend may need when things were not going well, or she could raise the roof at a house party. She could be like a calm spring morning, or she could be the eye of a hurricane. Either way, Laney was Laney. She was beautiful both inside and out. She was a friend, a daughter, a sister, and a role model who was taken away too soon. Her death hit deep into the souls of those who knew the true Laney Gwinner.

One of Laney's friends changed her birthday and refused to celebrate it on December 10th, because it fell on the same day as Laney's disappearance. Aby refused to celebrate her eleventh birthday because Laney wasn't there. Other friends stopped going out to places like Cheyenne Cattle Company because the place seemed dark without her. Others named their children after Laney because they felt it was the best way to keep her alive in their hearts.

Laney's legacy will live on for a long time. Laney wasn't perfect, but she was perfectly Laney.

# 5

# Family Matters

**"I find the family the most mysterious and fascinating institution in the world."**
— Amos Oz

*FAMILY* HAS A DICTIONARY DEFINITION, but we all see family in many different ways. Some families are extremely close, seemingly incapable of bad feelings, and always in the presence of one another. Some families are close spiritually or connected not by physical presence, but always in each other's hearts. Others appear dysfunctional, always yelling at each other or not speaking because of some argument from the past. No matter how close or separated a family may be, it is your family. The lasting impact on your life is undeniable. The lessons learned from your family, good and bad, are lessons carried into your future. The way it affects the future, however, is based on how the individual reacts, processes, and passes on those lessons.

In history, we see often that family dynamics can continue through generations, passing those values down the line. Too many times we see the abused become the abuser, the child of an alcoholic become the alcoholic, or the product of drug addiction become the drug addict. We also see the heroic acts of public servants who help their children having children who grow up to serve others. We see the God-fearing emotions of the faithful passed on to those kneeling to pray. The family is our outline of life. Do we always follow the outline? No, but it's there for us to go back to if we begin to stray or if we know that rewriting the outline is important.

Can families be both graceful and tormented at the same time? Yes. As a matter of fact, most are. We are human, and humans are definitely not perfect, so neither are families. One day the strength of the family bond is overwhelming, and the next day, frustration and anger can seem unbearable. In both situations, the one thing that stays constant is LOVE. Even in those families that don't work, love is in there somewhere; it just seems hard to find. In some families, LOVE is blind, so seeing the flaws of your family is sometimes hidden from reality because your family could do no wrong. Often, LOVE is brutally honest and tells you exactly what they think, feel, or observe in you. In almost every family, LOVE can be broken at times by those closest to you, but if someone outside the family tries to hurt a sibling, cousin, nephew, niece, parent, or grandparent, then watch out, because your family is coming up behind you and they have your back. Family matters. Family is your guide. Family is your future. Family is your safe space. Family can be great. Family can also be your obstacle. Family can be your uncomfortable space. Family can be troubling, but no matter who they are, family matters.

Everyone's experience is different. I cannot speak for anyone when it comes to their familial exposure, other than my own. I have a wonderful family. It hasn't been without jealousy, turmoil, arguments, and all the other things that come with a family, but it has also been supportive, focused, loving, and most of all cherished. Are we the perfect family from television shows like *Happy Days*, *The Andy Griffith Show*, and *The Brady Bunch*? Hell no. Do we have each other's backs? You better damn believe it. I, by the grace of God, have lived a tremendous life with my family and thank Him every day for what He has given me.

I know not everyone has that same luxury, and sometimes family can be found outside your biological connections. Sometimes teachers, coaches, neighbors, and many other people who come into a person's life when they are most impressionable can often fill a role that person feels they lack in their lives. The new role model can be a comforting soul that sees when they are upset, hungry, or angry, or they can be that authoritarian that gives them the discipline they may perceive as missing from their lives. Either way, it can be a wonderful experience for both involved.

There was a young man back in Kansas who saw me as that figure in his life. I was his football coach, and I was tough on him, but I also knew there was something missing in his life. He needed someone to set him straight when he needed it and someone to pat him on the back when he did something great on the field, but most importantly off it. He was a mentally tough kid, but you knew there had to be a reason for his maturity and for the occasions when his immaturity broke through. Sometimes I heard him tell his buddies after a game that he couldn't go with them to celebrate because he had to go pick up his little brother. I also saw him leave quickly after practice on some days because he had to go take his mom to work or to a doctor's appointment or something of that nature. I began to realize he was the man of the house, so to speak. Other days he would stick around for quite some time after practice, so I asked him what was up. He stated he wasn't ready to go home. His home life wasn't violent or anything like that; it was not the best for him. His real father was not around, and he didn't seem to gel with his stepfather, so going home sometimes was not as good as staying at football practice as long as he could.

For a short period of time during his day, I was that male figure he was missing. I let him know when he was not performing at his best and also gave him all the credit he deserved when he was. Was I his fill-in dad? No, not at all. He still had to go and face the truth in his home every night. His attitudes and his character were still being molded by his family. There is no escaping that. But sometimes others can help along the way. One thing I mentioned earlier is how a person interprets the lessons learned from their family, and this young man grew into an outstanding adult. He still tries to take care of his brother and mother because that is who he is, but he also tries to be the best father he can be because he did not necessarily get all that he needed from his own father or stepfather. He is successful and hard working. I am still close with him today nearly thirty-three years later. I see him as part of my family, maybe even that son we did not have. But his real family still molded him.

My point from this story is that family is always there one way or another. People can look for others to fill emotions that seem to be missing, and it can be a tremendous help, but your family is what causes you to be who you are, good and bad. Laney was no different than anyone else. Her family molded her into the person she was. She grew up in a suburban, middle-class family in West Chester, Ohio. She had a father, mother, and an older brother who loved her dearly. Like most siblings, David, her older brother, would pick on her, tease her, and probably sometimes push her around a bit, but he wouldn't be a brother if he didn't. He also was her protector. He could mess with Laney, but anyone else better look out. She was his little sister, and he was not going to let anything happen to her. Even as they grew into their twenties, David and Laney would sometimes go play pool or go to the bar to hang out with each other and their friends. Naturally, as you get into real-world jobs and obligations, time spent together with your siblings tends to go down, but Laney and David tried to spend as much time together as they could. They had the normal sibling disagreements, but they had each other's backs no matter what.

The father/daughter relationship is usually a very unique one. Often, the daughter is the apple of the father's eyes and Dad is the physical, mental, and emotional superman in hers. He is the one she runs to when she feels Mom is being unreasonable. Laney's father was exactly that. He was her hero. Her shoulder to cry on when her heart was broken. Her protector when someone treated her poorly. He was also the disciplinarian when she started to slip out of line. Unless you are a father of a daughter, in my case two of them, it is impossible to describe the bond within your hearts. It is coming home when they are young and them running into your arms as if it is the first time they have seen you in days. It is taking a nap with them, cuddling on the couch. It is going to their events at school and sitting in the back so they cannot see you, but they find you anyway. It is many sleepless nights waiting for them to come home. It is wanting them to be independent, but not so independent they don't need you anymore. It is wanting to protect them from anything that will hurt them either physically or mentally. The hardest part of being a girl dad is knowing you cannot be there every single minute of their lives.

It was no different for Mr. Gwinner. He was a dad who would do anything for his daughter, but he was a busy man. He was a very intelligent man who worked as a chemist for Procter & Gamble and later for an adhesive chemical company, Henkel Chemical. He worked hard and was a role model for his son and daughter. He emphasized the importance of having a strong work ethic and internal drive. He was the family provider. He made sure that David and Laney had what they needed. Not necessarily what they wanted, but what they needed. The unfortunate part of his job was the long hours and travel associated with his work. He was often gone from home, and this had an effect on both the children. For David, it meant that many of the roles of the man of the house fell upon his shoulders even at a young age. For Laney, it was difficult for her to find someone to see her side or to be there to lean on when she had a bad day.

When her father would come home, she did what most young girls do. She would run to him with a huge hug and spend the next few hours telling him about her day. For Laney, it was special when "Daddy" was home. It was her time to feel that special love that most fathers and daughters share. It was a time to feel that comforting hug and listen to his words of wisdom.

As she and David got older, they began to notice that their father was spending more and more time away from the house. He seemed to be working extreme hours or traveling a great deal. During those late teen years, David and Laney would begin to spend more time away from home as well. They would spend nights with friends even in the middle of the week. Unfortunately, Dad's reach of discipline was too far away when he was traveling, and like most kids, Laney and David began to venture out on their own, testing the waters of independence.

When she moved out on her own, she would even write in her planner when it was time to go see Dad, because she would always be "Daddy's Little Girl."

Moms love their sons, but a little girl is something they adore. The little girl who will grow up to be a beautiful, successful, and independent young woman. The girl who will wear the pink bows in her hair and the dresses that are so cute. The little girl that will be the image of herself. The hard work of a mother often goes widely unseen by most who see the family dynamics, but moms are special to the family, too. Laney's mom was no different. She would probably be upset with me right now because throughout this book I have referred to her daughter as Laney, instead of her given name of Alana. To her, Alana was her true name because it described the beauty she saw in her each and every day. She corrected Detective Smith on the name he used on the billboards placed all over town. She refused to allow him to call her Laney; it had to be Alana "Laney" Gwinner. That is her name and don't get it wrong. As I write this book, I feel as if maybe I should apologize to her for using the wrong name so often. Mrs. Gwinner was a momma bear, and if you had any ill intention toward her baby girl, you better watch out.

Like many mother/daughter relationships, it wasn't always hugs, kisses, and happy greetings for Laney and her mother. Daughters try to test the waters as much as they can, at least from what I have seen with my daughters and their mother. Mom is almost always right, but it takes the daughters a little longer in life to understand that. Often, what daughters don't see is that when things get bad, dads tend to be pretty heavy handed, but moms, even though they show a tough exterior, will stand by their daughters and redirect their fathers' anger. Laney was no different with her mom. She didn't always agree with her, and sometimes arguments seemed to be the norm for the day. There were many fights with loud voices and slamming of doors, but like almost all children, Laney would start to see the positive role her mother played in her life. She would also come to understand there was something else about her mother that she would have to grow a bit older to sympathize with.

In the 1980s and '90s, mental health was usually not discussed and oftentimes not treated as a medical condition. Going to a therapist wasn't exactly something you told others about; sharing your feelings was looked upon as being a bit weird. Growing up in that time period meant your parents were brought up in the 1950s. They were the children of The Greatest Generation. They were tough. They were strong. They were independent. They were not full of emotion. You did what you were told or oftentimes you had to pay the consequences. That didn't mean they didn't love you; they absolutely did. But they wanted you to be able to stand up against the world on your own. Behind closed doors, they felt the pain and disappointment you felt that comes with growing up; they didn't always show you. If someone was suffering from a type of mental illness, you hardly ever knew about it. Sometimes families would hide those with mental illness so that others wouldn't ask questions or wonder what was wrong with them. It was the silent generation, until you couldn't hide it anymore.

Unfortunately, for David and Laney, hiding their mother's mental illness was becoming more and more difficult. Sudden outbursts in the house or the cluttered rooms seemed normal, until they weren't. David and Laney would spend a great deal of time at other people's houses or stay away until it appeared things were getting better. Sadly, that didn't always work, as David would get a call to come get his mother from a local store because she was having an episode. Many of the people who knew her realized her illness, so often they called David, Laney, or Mr. Gwinner to come retrieve her. It was becoming a tough battle for all of them, especially Mrs. Gwinner. She often felt alone because others found it hard to stick around. Mr. Gwinner spent a great deal of time away from home, and sometimes David and Laney would purposely get out when they could and stay away as long as they could—sometimes leading to a wild night out. But they loved their mother, and she loved them. In Laney's time of need after a bad relationship or some other distressing incident, Mom was there to welcome her home until she could get back on her feet. Mrs. Gwinner was fighting a battle every day, but through all her ups and downs, her kids were still her greatest joy. Laney would jokingly write in a birthday card to her mother, "Love you mom! From your favorite daughter." After she moved out, Laney made time to make sure to go see her mother when her schedule allowed it.

As we looked at Laney—sorry, Mrs. Gwinner, Alana—during our deep dive into who she was, we had to look at everything. Work, play, friends, enemies, and family all have a role to play in your thoughts, actions, relationships, and routines. Laney loved people to a fault and wasn't afraid to show that, but she also was guarded because she didn't want to be hurt. She would go to the end of the world for people until they made her change her mind. She was a free spirit, always appearing to be looking for something. Was she independent because she had to be at a young age? Was she looking for love from a man to fill a void from Dad being away so much? Did she spend so much time away from home to avoid what she would encounter at home? We can only speculate. We will never know these answers, but what I will tell you is that, even though it wasn't always rainbows in her home, there was always love.

While looking into Laney's story, I have spent some time

talking with David. He is a great man, with a wonderful family, but you can tell there is still a huge hole in his heart. As I have been writing this book, I have been sending him excerpts for his approval. Sometimes it has taken him a long time to respond. I understand that life gets in the way. It's taken me two years to write this book because life has thrown me a couple of curve balls myself, but David always finds time somewhere along the way to respond. His last response to me while writing this hit me really hard and painted the perfect picture of what a family goes through when a loved one is needlessly taken from them. It has been twenty-seven years since Laney went missing, and it has taken its toll on the Gwinner family. David, in an email about Chapter 4 of this book, generously complimented me on my writing and teaching skills and apologized for not getting right back to me. I didn't understand his apology, but I did get a glimpse of what he goes through whenever Laney's story is brought up. He wants to help so badly, but it is not easy for him:

I have to get my mind right when I read these things. There have been so many years, so many articles, and so many conversations that I sometimes just need to step back and catch my breath before I start reading or talking about her again.

As I read this, I could actually feel his pain. It brought me to tears. I actually felt terrible that I had brought up the idea of writing this book about her because of the pain it causes David every time we talk. He not only has to re-live what happen to Laney, but what happened to his family.

The struggle I have with going back to the stories and conversations is not just the murder itself. I watched both of our parents die a very slow and painful death as a result.

The fallout after a loved one dies is difficult for any family, but to lose a sister and daughter to murder has got to be pretty unbearable. Survivors' guilt starts to set in, and all the what ifs continue to haunt every thought. David and Laney's dad took it extremely hard. He had to live with the guilt of not being able to protect his little girl. David continued:

My father spent almost the next decade (9 years) until [his death on] September 3, 2006 blaming himself for not protecting her better. He drank himself to death…

THE EERIE PART OF THAT STATEMENT THAT HE SENT ME WAS IN parenthesis. He put "(this very month and day)." I had sent him an email asking for his approval of Chapter 4 on the exact day that his father had died eighteen years prior. What was the chance of that happening? I didn't know if I should feel bad about that or maybe I was supposed to do it on that day to honor him.

Mrs. Gwinner, even though she was fighting her own battles, never gave up on trying to find answers to who took her baby. She focused on pushing the authorities to do more. She wrote letters. She took notes. She made phone calls. As time went on, her fight to find justice faded and her fight within herself began to take over. Her letters began to slip further and further from reality as she slipped further and further into depression.

She struggled more and more over time with depression until she passed on November 28, 2015. Watching her slip farther and farther away from reality in some of her letters… she became extremely depressed and paranoid. She ultimately gave up.

DAVID WENT ON TO TALK LOVINGLY ABOUT HIS FAMILY, BUT toward the end, you could feel a bit of anger start to creep into his writing. He spoke of why it was so hard for him to talk about Laney, the murder, and his parents:

So when we are talking about Laney's murder, I'm really talking about two other lives that the murderer took as well. The ones that are almost never mentioned, our mother and father. Really, they both kind of died that day the police officer came to the house to verify the body that was found in the river was my sister.

I know that David is doing well these days, but after reading what he sent me, I also feel a part of him died with the loss of his sister, mother, and father. He is a strong man, but it is clear that he lives with the pain of those losses every day. With the help of his wife and kids and the fond memories of his family, he carries on until one day he will meet them again. His mom is still writing those letters, but maybe through me this time. His dad is now holding his little girl, knowing she will never have to suffer again. And Alana "Laney" Gwinner is embracing them both for eternity. Through thick and thin, through good and bad, through life and in death, FAMILY MATTERS.

# 6

## Nature's Illusionist

**"I'm just waiting for people to start asking me to make the rain disappear."**
— David Copperfield

IT'S weird where and when things hit me as I dive deep into the case and sit to write a book about it. I'm writing the beginning of this chapter at a diner in Augusta, Georgia, called the Metro Diner. I'm sitting on a bar stool that is way too far away from the counter for my short legs, but that is a personal issue, I guess. As I look behind the counter into the kitchen, I see the hustle and bustle of the cooks working so hard to get the orders right and get them out in a timely manner, each concentrating on their part. It's controlled chaos, but the orders keep coming out like they have done this for years. As I look at everyone, I wonder what's going on in their heads and in their lives. Are they happy? Are they sad? Are they having a good life or are they hiding something? Each person seems so focused on the task at hand, barely missing a beat.

Now, I'm a person who wants to believe all people are good and only those rare, truly evil people will do bad things. I hope in my heart that those who do evil will be exposed and easy to spot, but I know that is not true. Could one or more of those people working behind the counter or even those sitting next to me be hiding something wicked? Vile people lurk in that saying "wolf in a sheep's clothing." Maybe someone in this room is a wolf, but right now no one sees it.

In Laney's case, the wolf struck. He took her into the woods, eventually leaving her somewhere close to the river. One day we hope to shed the sheep's clothing to reveal the predator, but for right now we have to keep searching for clues.

The police involved in the investigation seemed to think the main piece of evidence is the car and its location. Like I said before, there most likely isn't usable evidence in the car after twenty-six years, especially if it was in a body of water, but its location will help narrow down those who would have access or knowledge of the area. So the search goes on. Unfortunately, because of time passed, manpower reduced, and no new leads, the search has slowed down over the years. Every once in a while, a news story will flash across the television screen or on social media that shows a vehicle that has been found in one of the rivers or bodies of water in the area. With each new story, Laney's family, friends, and others who have followed the case hold their breath. The praying hands emoji or words of hope such as "please be the car" start to fill the social media screens, but time after time the rough current of disappointment pulls the life vest of hope away from their drowning hearts. Since her death, there have been a few vehicle discoveries that yielded answers to some secrets, but none for Laney.

When finding the car became the focus of the investigation, we looked at the Google Earth images of Fairfield, Ohio, starting from the bowling alley and expanding outward. Laney was found in the Ohio River, so we had to figure out how she could get so far down the Ohio River from Fairfield. As a crow flies, the bend in the river near Warsaw, Kentucky, is approximately fifty miles from Laney's last known location. That does not include the winding rivers that surround the greater Cincinnati area, which includes the river near Fairfield.

We knew that she left the bowling alley sometime after midnight, but the exact time is still debated. We know that according to the autopsy report, she was killed somewhere between twelve thirty a.m. and one a.m., and she was found near Warsaw, Kentucky, thirty-one days later. The car was not found, so the perpetrator had to be able to either get it out of town shortly after she went missing or they were able to hide it for a bit until they could get her and the car to the river. I will say they did have a pretty long window to accomplish this before anyone was actually looking for Laney.

What kind of mindset was this individual in? Were they panicking or were they calm about their next move? Did they think about how they were going to get rid of her and the car or did they react on impulse? Did they tell themselves they had to get rid of her and the car in the river or did they think maybe they should separate her from her car? I've listened to police officers and FBI profilers talk about how they try to get into the minds of the perpetrators to help figure out what they might do after such an event. I have tried hard to do this myself, but I find it really difficult. I don't know if it is because I'm not trained enough to do this or if it's that I can't see myself ever being in that situation. In my heart, it is the latter. But I know it is an important thing to try to do if you want to figure out where this person went with Laney and her car. One thing we know is that she had to be put somewhere where the river could grab her and bring her into its tormenting current. That means the search has to start in places that will lead to the Ohio River.

Sergeant Ed Roberts of the Fairfield Police Department was put on Laney's case shortly after she was reported missing by her parents. He began by returning to the bowling alley to speak with the owners and employees to see what they remembered from that night. As mentioned earlier in this book, Laney was a rare diamond in the midst of gravel. She stood out to all who saw her that evening. With her shining smile and lighthearted attitude, she drew people into the bar and kept many of them there longer than they ordinarily would have stayed. Most could not remember exactly when she arrived, and almost all of them had no real idea when she slipped into the night. At that time, with nothing really to work with, the police had to determine the next direction to go. It was a concerning situation because a young woman with no apparent reason to run off had not come home yet. The usual persons of interest were being looked into to see if anything stood out about their stories, but unfortunately, nothing was coming to light. As each day passed, the fears became almost unbearable for all those wondering, "Where is Laney?"

It became more clear as each day went by. Laney was gone, and the chance of her walking back through the door was dwindling. The focus was changing to a possible recovery mission. Where could someone and their car disappear? The obvious places come to mind. They began checking ditches on the side of the road. Did she drive her car to an unknown location and pass out, then freeze to death? There are many ponds and creeks and the Great Miami River all within a short drive from the bowling alley. Could she have driven into the water on her own? Possibly, but it didn't seem likely. Calls were coming in from all over the area and even from different states, claiming they had seen the sleek black Honda Del Sol driving on the highway or on a street in a nearby town. Some claimed to see a woman in distress in the car with a man, while others said they saw her driving and she seemed happy. What was true? The police had to try to run down each call to see if there was any credence to their claims but came up empty each time.

As time went on, the number of calls diminished. Fewer people were connected to her story. Life was moving on as the attention to the girl who went missing from Fairfield started to fade into the shadows of time. New stories on the television and in the newspaper were garnering attention. Her friends and family could not let go, though, because their beloved Laney was still out there somewhere.

On January 11, 1998, all things would change. Laney was found floating in the rough, dirty waters of the Ohio River. Now we knew where she was, but the big question was how did she get there? As mentioned earlier, it was determined she was not alive when she entered the water. This rules out accident or suicide because in those cases, she most likely would have signs of drowning, which she didn't. The perpetrator had to put her in the river or close to the river for her to end up so far from home. If you were to look at an aerial view of Cincinnati and the surrounding areas, it would give you an eerie yet beautiful image of a spider web. The rivers, streams, creeks, and small brooks make up the silky threads that lead to the predator's lair. Where should the search begin? This was the question the police had to ask themselves.

I don't know what the best method to figure out where she was placed in the water would be at this point. Do you start from where she was found and work back toward Fairfield to find the most logical location, or do you start in Fairfield and work toward Warsaw, Kentucky? Through our digging for information, we do know that Sgt. Roberts did a search of the Great Miami River in an area near the Charles M. Bolton Water Plant with the help of a local landowner whose backyard was connected to the Great Miami River, and this man seemed to be an expert on the actions of the everchanging water. The problem with our research is that we don't know when this search was conducted. The question we are still trying to answer is whether Sgt. Roberts did this search before or after she was found. This will become important when we come back to the differing theories by the police and those of Ken Purcell and others who saw her body at the recovery. Was or was she not in her car?

The location where Sgt. Roberts searched is approximately seven to eight miles from Laney's last known location. This distance can be covered in two main ways. One is taking the back roads in the cover of darkness to arrive at that particular bend in the river; the other is going on the more traveled roads but still arriving at the same general area.

One day my daughter and I happened to be passing by the bowling alley, and I told her we were going to do a scientific experiment. I told her to start the stopwatch when I said go and stop it when I told her to stop. A bit confused, she asked, "What are we doing?" I told her we were getting into the car with Laney on that awful night, and we were going to see how long it would take the killer to get to the river near that water plant. We were performing this study at night, but it wasn't a Tuesday night in December around one a.m. Though the conditions were not exact, it would at least give us a general idea of how long it would take to get to that location. We took the more traveled route that evening. This path today has a few more lights to contend with, but we actually got lucky and didn't hit many of them along the way. It took approximately twelve minutes to complete that drive.

Later, while I was on a solo mission, I took the back roads to check the time and, believe it or not, it was almost exactly the same. But why was this area so important? Laney could have been put in anywhere. Why would Sgt. Roberts look here? It is the closest entrance into the local river system from the bowling alley. If someone is going to quickly get rid of a car with Laney in it, it would likely be there. Unfortunately, Sgt. Roberts did not find the vehicle in that area. Later, that location would be checked again by the Butler County Sheriff's Office, as well as by our little team of sleuths, to confirm it was not there.

The river is like nature's David Copperfield. The illusionist can make even the Statue of Liberty disappear and reappear right before our eyes. The river may be the best magician to ever exist. One day, the river can expose the secrets that lie on her floor, then in a flash cover them again, not to be seen for days, weeks, months, or even decades. The mystery of Mother Nature's power is amazing. She can cover the skeletons of the deep for years, then when the time is right whisper in the ears of the right person to bring riddles of the dark into the light.

In October of 2021, nature's magician, the mighty Ohio River, performed again as she spoke with her mystic voice to a local police officer saying it was time to reveal one of her deep secrets. A local police department and dive team worked together to detect and confirm there was a vehicle in the Ohio River near Aurora, Indiana. Finding a car in the river is not that unusual. As a matter of fact, in October of 2022, an environmental group, Living Lands & Waters, and the Hamilton County Police Dive Team, pulled six vehicles from the Ohio River in one day. Of course, I immediately contacted this group, and they informed me that a 1993 Honda Del Sol was not one of those found. One vehicle that was located that day by another group on the water did give some hope to Laney's case, even though it was not her car. It was a 1997 Nissan Pathfinder SUV. The Pathfinder had been owned by twenty-six-year-old Stephanie Van Nguyen, a mother of two young children who had gone missing in 2002.

In April of 2002, Stephanie and her children had seemingly disappeared into thin air. There were extenuating circumstances to this case. Stephanie had allegedly left a note at her home stating she was going to drive into the river. After her disappearance, a search for her vehicle did not yield any results. Almost two decades later, a local police officer who had not given up followed some leads and went back to the location where many thought Stephanie may have driven her car into the river. This time armed with new sonar systems, the shape of a vehicle was spotted. Divine intervention or Mother Nature's empathy, whatever you want to call it, something special happened. It was the right time to expose that secret. I am not sure why that officer continued to follow those leads, but for some reason it was the right time. I say this because we actually had a volunteer drive several hours to meet us to use his boat and sonar to look for Laney in that same area several months before they found Stephanie's car. Dustin Faul volunteered to help us look for Laney's car in the Ohio River based on information we had obtained. We literally passed over that exact spot where Stephanie's car was found and did not see it. I truly believe it was not meant for us to locate it. It was saved for that police officer who needed those answers.

The results of that finding were simultaneously heartbreaking and relieving for those looking for Ms. Nguyen all those years. In January 2022, it was confirmed that human bones found in the vehicle were in fact those of Stephanie Van Nguyen. One question about her disappearance had been answered, but one still remains: What about the two young children? There were no other remains found in that car, so what happened to them? I'm sure there are officers still working to answer that question. I bring up this story to show that if Laney's car is in the river, there is still hope that one day it will be uncovered to help answer the question of who may have put it there.

That is the big question nearly twenty-six years later. Is Laney's car in the river? It would make logical sense for the car to be in one of the rivers around the tri-state area of southwest Ohio, southeast Indiana, and northern Kentucky. Laney was found in the Ohio River near Warsaw, Kentucky, and with the fast-moving water, she would have traveled very quickly down the river.

We had to figure out how far she could travel to end up at that big bend near Sugar Creek. We had to establish timelines for the days she was missing until the day she was found to estimate how far she could have traveled. The furthest distance she could have gone on the Great Miami River was estimated to be no further north than the Knight's Bridge Dam just south of the downtown area of Hamilton, Ohio, and the furthest east on the Ohio River was most likely near the Meldal Dam, near Foster, Kentucky. She may have traveled a bit further on the Ohio River if her body could have passed through some locks and dams along the way, but she would have had to be able to get through those dams without notice or damage to her body, which was not the case. Even after being in the river for thirty-one days, Laney's body did not show the severe damage that would have occurred if she had passed over or through a dam.

Ohio River 99.5" Jan. 9, 1998  "Laney" found Jan. 11, 1998
Body found - Sugar Bay - Opening of Sugar Creek to Ohio River

If body pushed out 2hrs before discovery car
would be located Near Big Bone Lick State Park

4hrs = Between Belleview, Ky & Rising Sun, IN

6 hrs : Petersburg, ky & Aurora, IN

7 hrs = Lawrenceburg IN & opening of Great Miami to the Ohio River.

8hrs = Northbend, OH

9hrs = Marathon Petro

7 hrs = Railroad bridge over GM @ Ohio River 1.5 mile walk to Lawrenceburg, IN

8 hrs = Elizabethtown Bridge = Shawnee Lookout

9 hrs = Hooven, OH

12 hrs = Dayton, Ky

11 hrs = Mill creek into Ohio River near Old paper factory

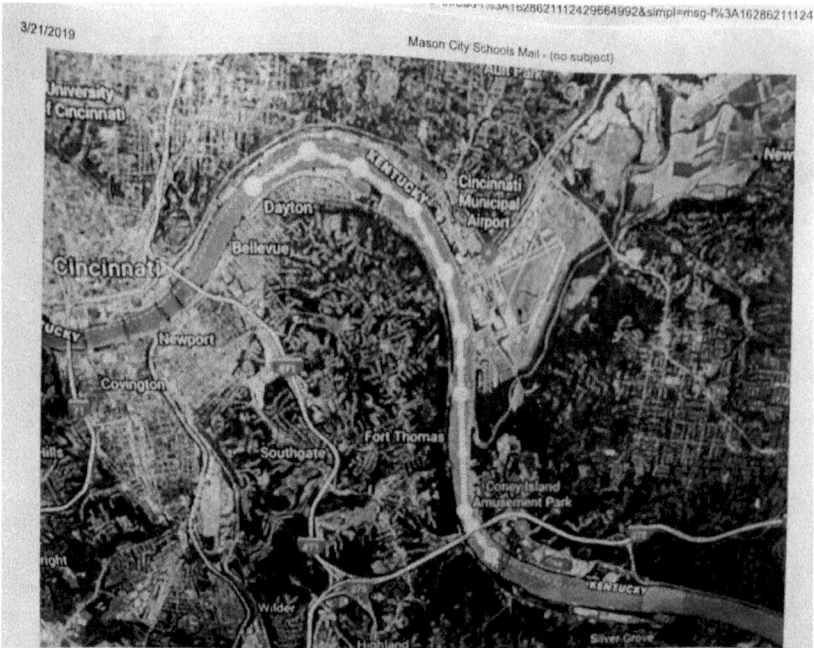

13 hrs 30 or 40 min = Coney Island/ Riverbend

— Baxter think there is something big on the River across from Coney Island

— Relevant to East side/Milford area

14 hrs = Silver grove, Ky

| 3/21/2019 Temperature (° F) | Florence, KY History \| Weather Under Max |
|---|---|
| Min Temperature | 33 |
| Precipitation (Inches) | Max |
| Precipitation | 1.62 |
| Dew Point (° F) | Max |

Mason City Schools Mail - (no subject)

7 hrs = Railroad bridge over GM @ Ohio River 1.5 mile walk to Lawrenceburg, IN

8 hrs = Elizabethtown Bridge = Shawnee Lookout

9 hrs = Hooven, OH

The low-head dams, as they are called, are extremely dangerous to small boats, kayaks, and swimmers if they get close to them, especially if the water is high due to rain. The low-head dam was designed to "raise the water level for improving municipal and industrial water supplies, producing hydropower, and diverting irrigation water," as stated by the Hannon Law Firm. Many of the smaller rivers around the area have several of these types of dams. If you watch a video or read about low-head dams, you will see why Laney would have had a great deal of damage done to her if she passed over one.

A low-head dam is known as a drowning machine. These dams can be from six inches high to twenty feet or more, and the water is designed to go over the top at a very high rate. When the water travels over the top into the river below, it immediately goes to the bottom and forces the water on the bottom to be pushed up to the top, creating a spinning motion similar to a washing machine. This large quantity of water is extremely powerful and has been known to snap gigantic trees that have been pushed over the top of the dam. The tremendous amount of debris in the river after a major storm rushes over these dams and tumbles over and over until the river decides it has had enough and pushes it out the other side. Place the body of a young woman in that tumbler with that debris and imagine the damage that would be inflicted upon her.

If we agree with the general premise that Laney was in her car and was driven into the river, then it limits the search area for that vehicle. Laney would have had to travel through the meandering river approximately thirty-three miles from the low-head dam in Hamilton, Ohio, to the delta of the Great Miami River as it flows into the Ohio River. If a person had to get rid of the car with Laney in it and had to do it quickly, what would be the most logical locations? The area had to be easily accessible but hidden as not to be seen. The location had to have a bank or ramp that was steep enough to get the car rolling so it would make it into the river. The location needed to be away from houses so that someone couldn't hear the car as it splashed into the water. If the killer used this as a way to dispose of Laney, then they must have known that, for the car to disappear, the water had to be deep enough. What locations would hide a car for a very long time? Much of the Great Miami River is very shallow, and often during dry summers, the river level will drop to expose things that have been dumped into it. As Evan, my student adventurer, revealed in a trip down the Great Miami in a kayak, there were several car frames and parts found on the banks.

There was even an almost fully intact Jeep found sticking out of the wall of the bank of the river. It had been covered for a very long time, but now it is not. The deepest parts of the river must be searched, but will those areas fit the other criteria to get rid of a car and not be seen or heard while doing so? Although there may be a few places that need to be re-examined, the police departments and our small group of Evan, a retired detective, a generous boat owner, and I have looked into these possible places of interest to no avail.

We did have one situation that seemed promising in the early months of 2018, when I received a phone call from a teacher in Mason County, Kentucky, informing me that he received a call looking for the teacher who was researching the Laney Gwinner case. The caller had seen the news story done by FOX19 News reporter Jessica Schmidt about the work that Evan and I were doing on the case. He was from southeast Indiana, which is close to Mason County, Kentucky, so he assumed Mason High School was in that area. Later in the book, I will talk about those people who wanted to help us find more information about Laney's case, but the information he gave us was pretty exciting. He informed us his uncle had been telling the police there was a sunken vehicle in the Great Miami River near his home for nearly twenty years. This was compelling because the location he described to us would put some of our people of interest in that geographical area. The location was about two and a half miles east of the Bolton Water Plant. It would take just a couple more minutes to travel down River Road to run the car into the river.

The only issue with this scenario is the perpetrator would be further away from the bowling alley. Would they be able to get back before being noticed? Did they have a separate car at the alley they would need to retrieve after getting rid of the evidence or did they walk across the bridge to a local establishment to call for help? So many unknowns for this part of the crime alone, but Evan and I had to take a look. We typed in the address into Google Earth to pinpoint its location, then hopped into our cars to head that way. Before we left, we called the Fairfield Police Department to let them know we were given this information and we were on our way to see if this was a legitimate lead. Was there really going to be a car there or was the caller merely wanting to be a part of something?

When we arrived, we pulled up to an old farmhouse that seemed to have seen its better days. There were several broken-down lawnmowers and rusted metal washtubs lying around the yard. We pulled into an old gravel driveway, not really knowing what we were going to encounter. Looking back, maybe we should have done a bit more reconnaissance to see what we were getting into, but to us, it was all about finding the car. When we got there, we parked our cars in front of an old barn that had the door partially closed and slightly hanging off its hinges. It had the appearance of one of those beautiful photos taken by a professional photographer, catching the old barn surrounded by overgrown grass and weeds, as if it has been forgotten in time. It was a serene feeling as if time had stood still and we were dropped into it. It was sunny and quiet.

Across the street was the remains of an old, abandoned factory that had been run by a large company that is very well known in the area. As we looked down the gravel road, there were two more barns, very similar to the first, but one had the door open. Suddenly, a dark black pickup truck made a sharp turn to get into the driveway, gravel dust impairing our vision. The truck pulled up to the second barn with a sudden push on the brakes. Evan and I looked at the vehicle, waiting for someone to emerge, but it seemed to be taking a while for them to exit. No one had come out of the house yet, and again, time felt like it was standing still. Were they going to take forever to get out of their car or house? Maybe we were in the wrong place. Oh shit, we wondered, what do we do if we pulled into the wrong driveway?

Eventually, a figure got out of the truck. He was an average-sized individual, about 5'9" or 5'10", of average build, about 170 or 180 pounds. When he got out of the car, we could tell he was a hard-working man. He had dirty blue jeans that looked as if they had a life story of strong labor to tell in those stains. He had a baseball cap on like a fella who had put a long day's work in and needed to go get a beer. He greeted us with a firm handshake and tired voice, but he wanted us to know he felt this could be something of importance.

While we shared our nods of thanks, a worn body appeared from behind the barns, and he walked up the gravel driveway. A man with long white hair and tattoos on his arms came strolling toward us. He was shirtless and had the appearance of a man who was one with nature. The thing that struck us the most about this man was the fact he was proudly walking up that gravel driveway with no shoes. Holy shit, my feet hurt just watching him, but he acted as if it was no big deal. He greeted us with a gruff voice that had a bit of skepticism in it, almost like it was bothering him that we were there. He shook our hands, then quickly gave us the hand gesture to follow him.

Evan and I weren't quite sure what we'd gotten ourselves into, but we were there, so we had to follow. Trying to make small talk with both of these gentlemen, we asked what they did for a living and how long they had been living there. The answers were short but to the point. We ventured down that long gravel road that seemed to go on forever. It was like that picture you see at arts and crafts stores showing a road narrowing into the mountains far in front of you. We passed the second barn to our left, then there was one more barn to the right. The door to that barn was open, and there was a beautiful John Deere tractor that had to have been purchased in the 1960s. Like most of the other stuff on that parcel of land, it had seen its better days. I was thinking to myself, *Holy crap, clean that thing up a bit and you could sell that for a fortune.*

At that moment, the nephew asked us to stop for a minute so he could go back to his truck and get something. No big deal, we could wait. We really were excited about the potential vehicle and changing the direction of this case, so we were willing to let this as long as necessary. While we waited, we engaged in small talk with his uncle. Come to find out he was a Vietnam veteran, and we thanked him for his service. Now the no-shoes thing made sense. As we turned around, we saw that the nephew had now started coming back toward us with a rifle in his hand.

You tell me what would be going through your mind!

We had been walking down a gravel road with people we didn't know, looking for a car that could be a part of a murder, in a place no one would know we were. Oh my God, what did I get us into? In my head, I wanted to tell Evan to run while I distracted them and to hope for the best. In reality, we both looked at each other and hoped that this was not a bad idea. Well, it wasn't. He was getting his gun because there were very territorial groundhogs in the area. He wanted to make sure we didn't run into one of them. Wait! Aggressive groundhogs? What the hell?! We continued down the road until it came to a bend, and the older gentleman said, "There it is."

Evan and I were standing about twenty-five feet above the river on a rocky bank, straining our eyes to see what he was talking about. The river was a bit high, but it was pretty clear at the time. Evan and I were still struggling to see when he directed us to move up a bit and look for the tires facing the surface of the water. I looked at Evan and said, "I see it. Do you?" He acknowledged me. Then we looked at the river and realized this might not be the best time to try to go out to the car. We marked the spot on the bank and asked the old man to contact us when the water got lower. The river has crazy power, and I didn't want to put any of us in danger.

Early June of that year, I got a call from the nephew telling me his uncle thought the water was low enough because he could see the tires peeking out. We had to form a game plan for how we were going to reach the vehicle in the river without putting ourselves in too much danger. Evan and I talked over the phone for a bit about the supplies we would need and how we were going to get in and out of the river from the bank. A small boat or kayak would have probably been a better approach, but we were not quite that smart. Our plan was easy to come up with, but the implementation wasn't simple. We had to first rappel down that twenty-five-foot bank to even get to the edge of the water. Okay, rappel may have been a little over-exaggerated, but we did have to climb down the steep grade that was covered in huge chunks of broken concrete that had been dumped along the bank to make sure the river did not eat away at the land. These slabs were pointing in different directions, some smooth surfaces facing downward to the water, others with their jagged edges sticking up inviting you to puncture your skin.

I purchased three rolls of three-hundred-foot nylon rope to tie around our waists but had to find something to anchor it to. As we looked around, we found a strong, sturdy tree at the top of the bank and secured ourselves to it. If you looked at us, you would think we were going to drop into a cave and dangle in the unknown darkness beneath us. The only thing we were missing were the hard hats with the flashlights on the front of them. Thinking back, a hard hat wouldn't have been a bad idea.

We started down the wall, moving slowly so as not to disturb any of the concrete slabs that may have been loose. It wasn't an easy trek, but we finally made it to the bottom. We could slightly see the shape of the car out in front of us but still needed to figure out the best way to get there. The old man told us that the water was shallow in most spots, but there were some deep pockets we had to watch out for. With the help of a telescoping painting pole, I began to poke around to find the best path to the car. Evan was following behind me, stepping on all the same uneven rocks and dipping into the same holes. At times, we were ankle deep, then the next step waist deep—well, my waist; Evan is taller than me, so maybe not waist deep on him. We eventually made it to the car. The tires were completely visible, but where was the rest of the car? As we braced ourselves in the rushing water, we blindly started reaching into the water to feel for the rest of the car.

There was the door.

There was the steering wheel.

There was the window.

There was the front bumper.

Oops! There was a large turtle skeleton.

There was the back bumper.

There was no license plate.

We continued to sift through the sediment, feeling our way around the car. We figured out it was upside down, so we had to orient ourselves to what we were finding. As we continued around the vehicle, we measured the distance from the front of the car to the back of the car, 160 inches. The width of the car was about sixty-eight inches. As we probed the frame of the car underneath the cloudy water, we took mental notes about what we could feel so that after we were finished, we could ask someone with expert knowledge of Honda vehicles if we had possibly found a Honda Del Sol. Our heart rates were beginning to race. Was this the car? Did we find what they had been looking for all these years?

As we would measure something new, we would yell up to the old man and his nephew, and they would respond back with a "Yep, that is the right size!" Was this old Vietnam veteran right all these years he tried to tell the police the car was there? Would this be the break needed to bring the wolf out of the woods? Did we do it? We knew the police needed to be contacted. Evan, being the genius he was, painted a plastic milk jug red and tied it to the car to mark it for them when they received our news.

We crawled back toward the bank, trying to remember the path we had taken to get out to the car. We moved slowly but had a bit of pep in our step. We needed to do some more research on what we had found and wanted to find the nearest spot where we could get a good cell connection to call the Fairfield Police Department and the Butler County Sheriff's Office. We scaled the concrete maze back up to the top of the wall, leaving a few layers of skin on some of those jagged edges. All four of us had a sense of accomplishment. Even if this wasn't her car, we at least put our efforts into a noble cause, and this location could be marked off for the search to continue in other areas. If it was Laney's car, it would hopefully bring some answers to her family and friends.

Excitedly, we walked back up that gravel road toward those vintage old barns, talking about what could be a major break in the case and possibly the end of some of the pain that had settled in the hearts of many for over two decades. The two gentlemen with us had an aurora of pride. They knew that what they were doing was right, and whatever the outcome, the old man could now rest easy because someone had listened and believed him about the car. We got to our own cars at end of the driveway. With a firm handshake and a nod of the head to thank them, we said our goodbyes and promised to stay in touch. Then Evan and I got into our car and pulled out of that old farmhouse driveway. As I looked in the rearview mirror, I saw the barefoot old man watching us until we were out of sight.

Excited about what we had found, we decided we needed to call Fairfield police and Butler County to let them know we found a car and it was marked for their easy recovery. We looked up the nearest Honda dealer because that seemed to be the smart thing to do and ventured in that direction. In our hopeful enthusiasm for finding the right car, Evan and I forgot what day it was. When we pulled into the Honda dealer, things seemed to be a little slow. Where was everyone? We didn't realize it was a Sunday evening and the dealership was closed. The only thing we had left to do was call the police.

The station phone rang and rang and rang, then someone finally picked up. "Okay, I got this," was nervously running through my brain. The phone picked up, and I began to feverishly rattle off the location, size, and possible make of the car before I realized it was like being on one of those crank voicemail messages that makes you start talking but the person is really not there. Disappointed, I realized I was talking to a recording. But with a proud voice, I gave the information like my brain had practiced it. Now all that was left was to wait for them to call me back.

A week passed, but nothing.

Four weeks passed, nothing.

Eight weeks passed, nothing.

The sounds of silence were deafening. The darkness seemed to be setting on Laney's case again. I was beginning to understand the frustration Laney's friends and family were feeling about what seemed to be the lack of interest in finding her killer. As my anger grew, I realized I needed to take a step back. Laney's case wasn't the only one the police were working on. We had no other focus, but the police departments did. It was easy to pass judgment when Laney was the only priority for us. We all unrealistically want to think that the police should be able to assign a detective to each case individually, at the drop of a hat, whenever new information, no matter how important it may be, is given to them. We expected them to stop what they were doing to jump to our beck and call. Reality set in, and we knew that we were going to have to wait to see what action would be taken. The police were busy and like the title of a future chapter, they were "Only Human."

The search had to continue, though. We sat down with Mark Reiber, a retired police detective we met through some really strange circumstances (which will be discussed later), to talk about our possibilities for future water expeditions. We needed Mark's detective experience to look at the maps again, to put ourselves in the shoes of the killer to figure out the most logical places that may have been used to dispose of the Del Sol. Gravel pits, ponds, lakes, and of course the river were reevaluated to make a list of those searched, those not, and those that maybe needed to be looked at again.

It would only be Mark and me because Evan had to work. Mark purchased an inflatable kayak so we could search some of the smaller bodies of water in the area. If someone was watching us two older gentlemen getting in and out of the inflatable, they would have had a great Instagram fail video to share with the world. We definitely were not very graceful in our endeavors, but we were determined. We had a small down-scanning sonar that was donated to us from Cabella's, and we were determined to find that car.

We put the kayak in the lake at the Thomas O. Marsh Park in Fairfield, which sits directly across the street from the Great Miami River, with the thought of the slim possibility the perpetrator may have tried to roll Laney down the bank of the river, then dispose of the car in this small lake adjacent to a neighborhood. Could the perp have then walked home? It was a long shot, but it was one we had to take. We rowed around the whole lake, looking for areas that may have been accessible for a person to put the car in the water, but no car was found.

We searched a pond in front of an apartment building that may have been a spot where a person of interest said he parked that night to sleep off the alcohol, but it was quickly determined that the pond was not deep enough.

The Fairfield area is dotted with many gravel and sand pits stretching down the Great Miami to the next county. Those gravel pits could have been a good place to hide a car, but again, how accessible were they back in 1997? As we looked back at the gravel pits using the time tool on Google Earth, we had to decide if the killer could have gotten in and out easily and whether a car would have been able to stay hidden all of these years. We checked one that would have been easy to get a car into, but we noticed the pit was too shallow for a car to have not been seen. Other gravel pit companies were called to see if their pits had been searched or dredged in the past. The ones we called confirmed that they were searched or dredged, confirming that the Honda Del Sol was still eluding us.

Individuals with the desire to help often find themselves connecting with others who have the same warm heart for those in need. While we were planning our next steps, we saw a news report of a man who found several cars in the Ohio River near Aberdeen, Ohio. In one of the vehicles, he found with his side- and down-scanning sonar the remains of an elderly man who had been missing for several years. We needed to find this Dustin Faul. Maybe he could help us find Laney's car.

The new mission for the moment was to seek out Dustin Faul, the man who could really give a boost to our search. Mark found Dustin—Dusty—and asked if he would be willing to help us. Without hesitation, Dusty said, "When and where? I will be there!" and the plan was set in motion. Early August of 2020, Dusty hitched up his boat to his truck and made the two-plus hour drive from his home in Aberdeen to Lawrenceburg, Indiana. We met at Tanner's Creek boat ramp to put his boat in the water and venture out onto the grand Ohio River in search of the secrets of the deep. Dusty moved efficiently to get his boat in the water. We engaged in small talk while he prepared the boat. I think we may have been a bit annoying to him as we interrupted his to-do list to make the boat river-worthy, but he wasn't going to let us know.

It was time to go, and Dusty was definitely in his element. That captain's seat was exactly where he belonged. We pushed off from the dock, slowly moving from the small, shallow creek toward the gigantic, deep waters of the Ohio. Once we were on the river moving toward our first stop, Dusty relaxed and began telling us his story. This will be discussed later in the book, but it made us feel good about what we were doing and that he was helping. The bumpy ride to our first search area was rough but serene at the same time. We slowly moved south along the shoreline, keeping our eyes on the sonar for anything that looked like a car. Mark and I had not seen a sonar like this before, and we were amazed that the images from the bottom were so clear.

There was a giant tree trunk. Was that a boat? We even saw what appeared to be a large bell similar to those used at the top of one of the many historical churches in the towns along the river. Unfortunately, we were limited on time, so we had to be specific about the areas we wanted to search. I actually had to get off the boat after a couple of hours because I had to return to school for a meeting.

After Mark and Dusty dropped me off, they continued north on the river toward the Great Miami River and Cincinnati. About two hours later, I got a picture texted to me from Mark. Then a message came in right after: "WE FOUND A CAR." I began to look carefully at the sonar picture.

At the time, Mark, Dusty, and WLWT5 reporter, Karin Johnson, were on the boat, and I was also in touch with Jessica from FOX19. Both reporters were extremely interested in the content of that picture. It was grainy, yet you could definitely see what appeared to be a small car with the door open. Was this it? Again, if it was, there was a person of interest in the geographical window of this drop area. It appeared to be in an place that would have been very difficult to get to the river, but after a bit more research, I found that in 1997 there was an access road to the local energy plant that went all the way around the corner of the river to where this image was found. The only thing to do now was confirm. How were we going to do that? We were not certified divers, and even if we were, diving in a river is much different than a lake or ocean. The current is strong, and the visibility is extremely low. Who could we get to help us?

Mark is pretty well connected to many of the authorities in the area. He contacted a friend of his on the Hamilton County Dive Team to see if they could help. The dive team routinely practices in the local rivers to always be prepared for any call they may receive. They informed Mark this would be a good opportunity to kill two birds with one stone. They'd get to practice and, hopefully, we'd get to identify the vehicle. Due to this thing called a job, I was not able to go with Mark and the team to see if it was a car. I was so disappointed! Then, in the middle of my day, I got a text that said, "We can't find the car."

What?

Did the river pull her magic again?

Did they miss the mark?

What happened?

Was this another dead end?

Was the magic of the river at work again? In our heads, we were trying to remember if it had rained lately. Did the river rise and deposit its sediment over top of the car? Did we not have it marked well enough? There were many questions about why it wasn't found, but we couldn't ponder for too long. We had to figure out the next step.

Evan took control. He began to look for other individuals who may be able to help us when he came across a group called Adventures with Purpose. This was a volunteer dive group that had a huge following on YouTube. They were called to places where individuals had gone missing in their vehicles and were presumed to have entered some type of water nearby. They started out as a group that recorded their adventures of cleaning up a river, but then one day they found a car at the bottom of it. They uncovered the license plate. Then, to their surprise, it appeared as if there was an occupant in the car. This started a movement to help find missing individuals based on information given to them about their last known location.

Evan noted that the group was doing a trip around the United States, and they were going to be in our area in September 2020. With the promise of buying them a famous Skyline Chili cheese coney, he was able to persuade them to come to Cincinnati to help us look for Laney's Del Sol. Apparently, the offer worked because within a day of contacting them a message came across our phones: "We are on our way."

Excited about the potential of using experts to help us find the car, we had to make a plan. The common thread of "time" popped up again. They were traveling across the country and had many stops to make. We had to be efficient and precise about the locations to search. Of course, we had to start where Dusty had taken that sonar picture. It looked too much like a car to not check again.

On a humid Saturday morning in September, the adventure with Adventure with Purpose began. We met at a local boat ramp near the Shawnee Lookout State Park. As a group, we discussed why this location was important and what would be the best way to reach that location, since the access road was gone now. The access road originally was connected to the local power plant station along the Ohio River. This would put us very close to the car. It seemed to be a good launching point for the small inflatable boat they used. Entering the driveway to the power plant, we thought there would be someone there to greet us and tell us if we could continue back to the area close to the river. It was strange because no one even stopped us. After the attack on September 11, 2001, security at power plants around the United States became very stringent, so getting through the gates without notice didn't seem right.

We started down a few gravel roads that eventually turned into a two-track gravel road, then the gravel disappeared and we were driving on an overgrown grass and dirt path. Not going to lie, I was waiting for the authorities to come barreling in, lights flashing and guns drawn. Okay, maybe I was overthinking it a bit, like I was Tom Cruise in a *Mission: Impossible* movie, but it was a bit eerie.

We arrived at what we thought was the best place to put the boat in when what I had imagined seemed to be coming true. Around the corner, moving pretty fast, was a marked security vehicle with the lights on. Oh shit! How am I going to explain this one to my school and my wife? Thankfully, they were not there to arrest us, but after we explained what we were doing there, they did ask us to leave immediately. Dejected a bit, but also relieved we weren't being arrested, we moved away from the power plant to come up with another game plan.

The next staging area was back at the boat ramp where we originally started. The new plan was that the Adventures with Purpose guys would inflate their boat at this ramp and then get into a small branch of the river that poked its way through the woods to the place we were standing. This turned out to be a pretty funny approach, but I will elaborate on that later in the book. We talked about the location of the possible car in the river and how those going to dive for it would meander their way there. Evan, in his kayak, would be the navigator tied to the motorized inflatable the dive team used. The rest of us would go back up to the road that meandered its way along the river.

We parked on a curve approximately 350 feet from the point in the river where we believed the car might be. The forest along the road is pretty dense, but we thought the walk wouldn't be that big of a deal. We were wrong. The walk was not a straight 350 feet. The terrain was rough and covered in trees, weeds, and tall grasses. It reminded me of that scene from *Forest Gump* when he had to run through the jungles of Vietnam to get Bubba out. One step you would be on even ground, then in a flash you were up to your hips in the tall grass. It didn't help that it happened to be one of the hottest days of the year. As we finally trudged our way to the bank, Evan and the inflatable were turning the corner on the river, coming right toward us.

The inflatable was designed by the diving crew to make getting in and out of the river easy, as well as to allow them to position the sonar in the best possible location to see the secrets at the bottom. At this point, they detached Evan so they could scan the area in the hopes of finding the car. The sonar would pick something up, then suddenly lose it. The crew circled the area several times until they finally zeroed in on what could be the shape of the car.

On this day, Adventures with Purpose had brought a new guy to see if he would fit the mold to be a part of their permanent crew. He suited up in his wet suit, goggles, oxygen tank, and his GoPro camera. He jumped into the water to acclimate himself for a few minutes before descending into the greenish-brown, murky water. While acclimating, he began to bounce up and down like a fishing bobber in the water, exclaiming, "I'm bouncing on the hood!" Again, excitement rushed through our veins. He then sank slowly underwater, the air bubbles bursting at the top. He had the ability to communicate with the crew chief, so he was giving him details of what he could see at the bottom. Visibility was not very good, and he estimated the most he could see in front of him was about three feet. He was underwater for about fifteen minutes, only to rise slowly like the creature from the black lagoon to tell us we were looking at a giant tree stump with its roots still attached. It goes without saying that we were deeply disappointed and frustrated once again.

We left there a little dejected, but we did promise to buy them the famous Skyline Chili. After lunch, the group could search a few more spots before they had to begin their drive back to the West.

Since I'm still writing about this, you might deduce that we did not find a car.

Sixteen weeks had passed since we contacted the police about the car in the river. Nothing.

Eighteen weeks had passed. It was around three thirty p.m. I had just gotten home from school and was about to take a nap when my phone rang. Exhausted, I almost didn't answer the phone, but I did. It was the old man's nephew.

"Hey, are you at my uncle's house?" he said.

"Umm... no, why?"

"The police are there, and they are pulling out that car!" he said.

"Seriously? Shit, I have to hurry up and get over there!"

I jumped off the couch and ran to the door as fast as I could. I grabbed my keys and wallet and sprinted out to my car. On a normal day, it would take me about twenty-five minutes to get to the old man's house. I'm pretty sure that I should have gotten a ticket because I made it there in about fifteen minutes. I spun my tires in that gravel driveway, then in one motion shut the car off and jumped out. I moved quickly, almost running, but I didn't want to seem too eager when I approached the tow trucks and police officers standing on the bank. I saw a man in a suit who looked pretty important, so I made my way over to introduce myself. With a firm handshake, I let him know we were the ones who called about the car. He didn't seem all that impressed but cordially said thank you and handed me his card. Curiously, I said, "Was it her car?" He looked at me with little emotion and said, "No." That was it. Just "No." Well, crap! The enthusiasm was sucked right out of me again. Not her car.

An illusionist has used sleight of hand to hide the deep, dark secrets of the past. The question is who was the magician? Was Mother Nature deceiving us for a little longer or was the true wizard the killer, who for twenty-six years has hidden the one thing that will bring him out from behind the curtain? Unlike a true magician, I believe this imposter has told someone the way he accomplished his trick.

Soon your secrets will be out. One day, whether it is uncovered by the river's grace or through the mouth of someone you trusted, you will be exposed. The hand is quicker than the eye, but the mind is stronger than the magic. We will eventually learn how the illusion was performed and bring you out of your sheep's clothing.

The search continues…

# 7

## Monsters Among Us

**The wolf hunts a hungry man and the devil a lonely heart… I keep my faith intact, make sure my prayers are said 'cause I've learned that the monsters ain't the ones beneath the bed.**
—Eric Church, "Monsters"

AS YOU LIE in bed at night, especially as a kid, you often stare at the window, letting your mind run wild with what might be outside that glass. The imagination runs movie clips of *Friday the 13ᵗʰ* with Jason Voorhees staring back at you in the reflections. The eerie sounds of the owl hooting from the trees instill a bit of fear in your gut. You look away and cover your eyes, then look back quickly to see that nothing is out there. I'm not gonna lie, I still have those thoughts go through my mind sometimes. The dark can be scary, but eventually, we realize that most of those fears are ridiculous. I'm in my home; nothing is going to hurt me. The sun rises and those monsters of the dark fade away with the bright morning light.

Here is what is disturbing to me. Those awful feelings show up in the safest of places: your own home. For some reason when the darkness is outside, we fear it, but if we are outside with it, the fear doesn't seem as bad. Outside is actually where we should be a bit scared and pay attention to our surroundings. When we are outside, we feel empowered and bulletproof, but we see every day on the news the heinous crimes committed by sick individuals. As singer Eric Church says, "The wolf hunts a hungry man and the devil a lonely heart." The wolf in sheep's clothing with its devilish heart is anxious to pounce on unsuspecting prey. Laney was no different than what most of us would have been that night. She was a strong woman, out to have some fun. A few drinks with a friend to celebrate an achievement and then get into the arms of someone she loves. The walk to the car wasn't that far. She'd be okay. We have all done this a million times. I know my wife has done this at times even when I'm available to go with her. That short walk to the car is no big deal, until it is. The demons of the dark hide everywhere, and when they are ready to creep out from the shadows, they will.

Earlier I mentioned that it was weird when and where thoughts creep into your mind. I digress back to the Metro Diner in Augusta, Georgia, thinking about all those people working there or eating around me. What don't we know about those around us? Who is the wolf? Who has the potential to change in a second? Unfortunately, those wolves are around us every day and we may never know it. But if we ever find out, it could be bad. Some will snap and go after a large group of people, while others lurk in the shadows, waiting for their opportunity to strike out at that one unsuspecting victim. Some will stalk their prey, while others will seize the moment when it arises. Who is here with me? What is going through that person's mind right now? I'm not trying to scare people into not going out ever again. Ninety-eight percent of people you will encounter are awesome human beings that have true love in their hearts. All I'm saying is that no matter where you go people have secrets, and some people are like monsters waiting underneath the bed.

On December 9, 1997, at the Gilmore Bowling Lanes, in Fairfield, OH, there were many with pasts that were not exactly angelic. Now, no one is perfect and we all do stupid things when we are young, well, because we are young, but a few individuals that night had a little more to hide. Some were fighting demons of the past, while others were right in the middle of their struggles. Some were lonely. Some didn't care who they hurt. A few found themselves in the middle of the chaos to come merely because of who they were, and they weren't even at the alley that night. In the book *Solving Cold Cases: Investigation Techniques and Protocol*, Joe D. Kennedy and Hogan Hilling state the "correct suspect surfaces early in the investigation" (p. 27). They suggest that, when looking at cold cases, the person responsible for the crime will show up within the first thirty days of the original investigation (Kennedy, p. 27).

In this chapter, I'm going to talk about some of those people and explain why they are important to Laney's story. I'm pretty sure most of these individuals were spoken to at the beginning of the investigation, but one may have slipped through the cracks. Do I think one of them committed this crime? Yes, I do, but I'm going to let you decide that.

I will be changing some names of the individuals described in this chapter to protect their identities. No one has been arrested or named a suspect in Laney's case, and I don't want to impede the investigation or wrongfully create an image of someone who may be innocent. I will describe why I think they are important people to look into for Laney's death, but again, in no way am I accusing anyone at this time of her murder. I am simply stating the information that makes them a person of interest. I have spoken with several retired police officers about how to look at individuals such as these to determine the most logical one to consider, but I am not an expert, nor will I ever claim I am. These are just ideas based on what we know and what I have learned along the way. If anyone out there knows more information about individuals that should be considered, please contact the Fairfield, Ohio, Police Department or the Butler County Sheriff's Office with that information.

When looking at individuals who could have committed a murder, you first have to look at the victim. This is known as victimology. Victimology is the in-depth look into the person upon whom the unlawful act was perpetrated. Who was Laney? What about her prior to that night and on that night would make her susceptible to abduction and murder? Here is where some people think we are trying to blame the victim for what happened to them. That is absolutely false. This is simply the process the investigators have to go through to find out what the one thing was that may have changed or could have triggered someone to pick her as their victim. The person who kills someone is always to blame for their unspeakable actions, but figuring out what caused those two individuals to cross paths at that time, place, and circumstance is the aim of victimology.

Studying Laney's patterns, financial status, love and relationships, and her future goals is tough to do two decades after her disappearance. Records are not easily accessible, and coworkers and friends can only remember the warm memories of Laney in those deepest parts of their hearts and souls. Some individuals who may have known more about the details of her life are either so bothered by her death they do not want to speak about it because it is too painful, or unfortunately time has taken some individuals away from Earth to hang out with Laney in those beautiful, eternal fields of gold.

While looking into Laney's case, I had the opportunity to meet with one of the most impressive women I have ever met. Dr. Laura

Pettler, the CEO and founder of Laura Pettler and Associates (LPA) Death Investigations, has spent much of her life researching the use of victim-centered death investigations. Dr. Pettler is a tremendous investigator with a determination to make a difference in the field of forensic science. In her book, *Crime Scene Staging Dynamics in Homicide Cases*, she uses Maslow's hierarchy of needs to help explain victimology. She references how Abraham Maslow (1943) used a taxonomy or "structure of interrelated components or variables where one builds upon the underlying level or levels" (Pettler). Maslow used this to explain how people progress through their lives by going through five stages of growth. Dr. Pettler used it to explain how those same five stages could help develop a picture of who a person was before the crime was committed in the hopes that a break in a pattern could give insight into what a perpetrator encountered that particular night to make them commit the murder. The hierarchy includes everything from simple demographics, like ethnic background, height, weight, hair color, eye color, and general build, to the complexities of love and belonging and what the meaning of life was supposed to be in her mind.

Like my wife always tells our daughters, "Every person's path is different," but every person's path can also be traced over time and analyzed to see where they may be headed. Laney had traveled her own path in her short twenty-three years, weaving in and out of the highs and lows of basic needs—love, money, family, and looking toward future endeavors. She was surging toward a successful business career but still fought the financial lows common to many twenty-three-year-olds. She had a loving family but not without turmoil. She was searching for Mr. Right but seemed to be looking in the wrong places. She was showered with attention from friends but sometimes seemed to be lonely. She was small, kind, and beautiful but could stand her ground and take on any giant if need be. She was the one and only Alana "Laney" Gwinner.

The process of gathering the information on Laney to fit into this hierarchy was a difficult task. As mentioned earlier, it has been two decades since her murder, and like old pictures in a box in the attic, time tends to discolor and blur the images. Evan and I tried to dust off those old boxes to see Laney a bit more clearly. We needed to do our best to try to put her life back together as neatly as possible to find that missing piece of the puzzle that always seems to get lost under the table, leaving a hole in the final picture. I don't think we found that, but we did find some that could possibly fill in some of the puzzle. However, until her case is solved, there will always be that annoying hole. For Laney, the Maslow puzzle doesn't fit neatly together.

The next step is to look carefully at the scene to determine many aspects of that particular crime. Location, time, evidence, type of crime, and type of victim are all major points to consider when trying to determine what type of person would commit such an act. I know that there is far more that goes into this section of the investigation, but the details are immense, and in Laney's case they are hidden very well. Where exactly was the crime scene? The bowling alley is most likely where the crime began, but was there actually an unlawful act committed there? It did not seem, from witnesses, as if someone grabbed Laney right out of the bar and forced her to the parking lot. If someone was able to force her out of the alley, then they were very stealthy, because no one seemed to even know she left, even her friend, Shad. Laney didn't appear to be the type to allow someone to force her to do anything. I think, if she was capable, she would have made a scene or created a distraction of some sort to draw attention to herself. Abducting her from inside the bowling alley would be a bold move, and I don't think the individuals there that night would have taken that chance. The attention was already on Laney, so her leaving with someone would have been noticed. It is likely she was able to slip out because she wanted to leave on her own.

This leads to other questions about the killer:

Was the killer already outside?

Did they know she was planning to leave and were lying in wait?

Were they in the parking lot for some unknown reason and took advantage of the opportunity?

Did she leave by herself to meet someone and things got out of hand?

Did she actually leave alone or did she leave with someone she knew?

Unfortunately, we may never know the answers to these questions. The only thing we can do is speculate about what happened after she slipped into the neon shadows of the bowling alley sign. The crime scene is unknown and, according to those who worked on her case, evidence is very limited.

In all cases, those closest to the victim are the first to be investigated. This seems to be common sense, but there is actual data to support this train of thought. In a 2011 report presented by the U.S. Department of Justice, Bureau of Justice Statistics, the percentage of homicide cases in which the victim knew their killer was 78.1 percent of all the murder cases reported to this study. Think about those numbers: out of one hundred people murdered, seventy-eight were murdered by someone they knew. Wow! To me that is a crazy number. I know we see this every day on the news, but in my heart I would hope that people you know would never be able to do something bad to you. However, I know emotions are strong, and sometimes those we hurt the most are those we love the most. While looking at those statistics, I thought the greater number of those known murderers would be boyfriends, husbands, ex-boyfriends, and ex-husbands. I know this sounds male heavy, but the study also showed that males tend to be the perpetrator of most violent crimes. To my surprise, the stats actually show that about half of those murders were committed by mere acquaintances, which included friends, friends of friends, and people a person may have only met a few times.

How did Laney's victimology intersect with individuals that could have possibly committed her murder? Which one of them could have been the wolf I have been referring to throughout this book? I will try to describe the people we believe were present that night and the reason we feel their connection to Laney could have been deadly. Again, some names have been changed to protect those individuals' rights, but we believe most of the information about them is accurate.

Laney had reached a goal by completing her associate's degree in business and wanted to celebrate with her friends. From what I know about her and her friends, it didn't necessarily take an accomplishment to want to have some fun, but it was a good reason to get together. The emails started early in the week about when and where this celebration would take place. Laney started spreading the word, and at first many of the friends were all about getting some food and adult beverages. Unfortunately, as the short week progressed, multiple friends had to bail out for various reasons. It was a Tuesday night, so it wasn't exactly the most convenient night to get shitfaced drunk, because even though Laney and her friends were young, attractive, and didn't need much of an excuse to party, they did have jobs, families, and general responsibilities to attend to. As stated before, one had a sick child, and maybe a bit of a conscience about going out in the middle of the week. Another became sick, while others in retrospect couldn't even remember why they couldn't make it. But Laney was determined to celebrate her accomplishment, and I don't blame her. At twenty-three, the world is confusing because having fun is still a priority, but adulting is knocking on the door, and she was starting to put her life in order.

The evening started at Buffalo Wild Wings near Forest Fair Mall. Laney arrived to meet with one of her friends, Shad. Shad was an acquaintance from the line dancing and rodeo crowd Laney spent a great deal of time with. According to some of the emails sent to Angie, Shad had been missing from the group for a while. His absence was because of a woman. That woman was also a member of the group, and they—or should I say she—had recently decided that things were moving a bit fast and possibly taking a little time apart would be good for the relationship. When Laney invited her friends to the celebration, Shad was on the list, and he decided it was time to step out again.

The unique connection between Shad and the group was his best friend EJ. The group of friends would later describe EJ as the LOVE of Laney's life. The one that almost got away. When Laney went missing and didn't show up to her boyfriend's house, the first thought to cross the minds of her friends was that Laney had run off to see EJ. EJ had actually stated that he spoke with Laney that morning, and he admitted he felt as if they would one day get back together. We will talk more about EJ in this chapter, but as far as we know, he was out of town that night. Would Laney have run to meet EJ? We don't know. It could be something to look into. However, we must first start with Shad.

According to the information found, Shad was supposedly the last person to see Laney alive, so naturally we have to look at him as a person of interest. Who was Shad? Shad was also on that path between crazy dreams and the reality of having to work for a living. He worked for a local waste management company during the week, while venturing out on the weekends to chase the gold buckles of the rodeo. From what I gathered from a friend of mine involved in the rodeo business at the highest level, Shad was probably chasing a dream beyond his ability. He was described to me as an "all right" bull rider but wasn't exactly going to be featured in a Professional Bull Riders Association event. Shad was perceived as the sidekick to EJ. Did that make Shad feel a bit overlooked? EJ was an athletic, bulky individual, often seen as a bit intimidating, where Shad was not exactly perceived as a physical presence. Like most individuals in their twenties, Shad may have been trying to find that person to complete his emotional life but had not found them yet.

Shad was the only one with Laney that night. As the night went on and the drinking continued, many witnesses described the interactions between her and Shad seeming to get more affectionate. Most had said they perceived them to be a couple, even some describing a great deal of hugging and kissing. As a twenty-something single male who had just come out of a relationship, how would you respond to that? I think you get the picture.

Was there an alcohol-induced spark?

Did Laney give a signal that Shad may have taken to heart?

With EJ not there and the fact EJ and Laney were not seeing each other anymore, did Shad get the feeling the window was open?

Did Laney and Shad go to the parking lot and something went wrong?

Could Shad be suppressing the guilt of that night long enough to get through this life and hope for forgiveness at the gates of Heaven in the afterlife?

To Shad's defense, most of the people who witnessed the two that night said they believed that Laney left well before him. Some said they saw him having a drink with another male and Laney was not there. An acquaintance, not really a friend of Shad's, also told investigators they had seen Shad leave after Laney, then witnessed him warming up his truck through the large picture window in the front of the bar. Do we know all of Shad's actions? No, but we also have no proof that anything happened between him and Laney other than what was witnessed in the bar. Shad has gone on to live a quiet, normal life with no criminal record. He seems to be an asset to his community. He still has an interest in horses and the country life. Maybe his dreams of being a rodeo champion did not come true, but as for a life well lived, it seems to have gone pretty well.

But for some reason, I cannot shake him out of my head.

He was the last one to see her alive.

He had friends who are really not good people, and talking with Laney's friends, they seem to think Shad's friends would help hide something.

According to some, he never seemed very concerned about what happened that night.

Am I accusing him of this awful crime? Absolutely not! There seems to be no evidence linking him to what happened to Laney, but I cannot seem to let it go. I'm not sure why, but it keeps gnawing at my gut that he possibly had something to do with her murder.

The bowling alley and bar is a study in sociology. There are many different types of people all under one roof. The haves and have nots all together and most not noticing the difference between the two. There are social groups of similar people, as well as groups of completely different backgrounds, personalities, and attitudes. The things they had in common were the game of bowling and the cold beverages. The bar was a place for a nightcap to unwind after a night of bowling or a long day of work. For some, it was a chance to play some pool or darts and enjoy the company of friends. That night for everyone would be a night to remember. Many would be questioned about what they had seen that night, while others would have to endure a bit more scrutiny over time. Shad was the obvious first look, but who else would be pulled into the mystery of Laney's disappearance and eventual death?

Most who are intrigued with true crime know that those closest to the victim will be placed quickly on the radar of the investigation. As stated before, data has shown most victims of violent crimes knew their perpetrator. This means friends, family, boyfriends, and ex-boyfriends will all be thoroughly investigated to see who can be eliminated and who cannot. With no real crime scene plus the time she spent in the elements, the investigation is going to come down to someone either saying the right thing or the wrong thing, or a technological breakthrough with the limited evidence the police have. Until that day, we have to keep looking at those who cannot be completely eliminated.

Laney's last known phone call was to her current boyfriend of only about six weeks. Mike had been quoted in the media saying that Laney called and left a message saying she was on her way to his home. He lived less than ten minutes away from the bowling lanes. The call was supposedly around twelve thirty a.m. If she left right after, that would put her at his home around twelve forty to twelve fifty a.m. The actual time she walked to her car has not been pinpointed. Mike stated he was in bed when she made the call because he had to be at work early the next morning and he told her he would leave the door open for her. He fell asleep only to wake up the next morning to not seeing Laney anywhere in his home. Concerned, Mike called her place of employment to see if she had made it to work. When her work colleagues stated she was not at work, the anxiety of the situation began to rise. Mike seemed very concerned, which would point to his lack of involvement, but when looking at this case several decades later, some of the information about his actions after her phone call beg for further attention.

At the time, he was a fit, twenty-something man, and to many of Laney's friends, he was attractive. All who knew or met him felt he was a good guy with good intentions toward their beloved Laney. They met at a party in Kentucky and seemed to hit it off pretty quickly. The next several weeks they would be seen together at her friends' houses or at his house when his friends would get together to partake in some drinking and having a good time. That's what many do when in their twenties, work during the week to have fun on the weekend, which often started on Thursday. Relationships were fluid without full commitment because, let's be honest, most at that age just want to have sex. That period of life is difficult because you want to keep having that uncontrolled fun, but the reality is you have to grow up soon and you don't want to do it alone. Finding Mr. or Mrs. Right begins to creep into your mind, and the search for that forever relationship grabs hold of you.

Laney and Mike were no different. They wanted that ecstasy of the moment with no strings attached, but many of Laney's friends also knew that some of those strings may have been latching on. The relationship was still very new, so wedding bells were not ringing yet, but they were beginning to spend a pretty significant amount of time together. Both had recently gotten out of relationships, so I'm pretty sure they were not moving too fast, but again when a very beautiful young woman and a very attractive young man get together, sparks are going to fly.

The week before Laney's disappearance, she and Mike went to a work party, and from the pictures, they both looked pretty happy. Laney would later tell Angie that it went well and they had a great time. The weekend came, and Mike had some people over to his house. Laney would show up to the party looking, well, like Laney. The hot girl every guy wanted to talk to. This was her special power, but often it also became her worst enemy. Wherever Laney showed up somewhere, other girls who didn't know her immediately started throwing her looks that could kill. Laney turned the guys' heads, and there was nothing those girls could do about it. Many stories from her friends always seemed to start or end with a girl confronting Laney because their guy seemed to be more interested in her, and from what I understand, Laney wasn't going to take shit from anyone. This party was no different. While Mike was walking around being the good host, a female friend of his stepped into Laney's bubble to accuse her of talking with her man. In Laney's words to Angie in an email, she said, "[T]here was some yelling, but I was good." That interaction did spark a response from Mike, but I don't have all the details on what that was. Laney told Angie she would talk to her at BW's about his reaction and get her take on it, but unfortunately that conversation would never happen.

How did Mike respond?

I don't think his response was threatening at all. Laney did not express to anyone that it was more than him being upset that a fight almost broke out at his house. Did they argue about it? Maybe. But would that be a reason to upset him enough to kill her days later? I doubt it. I think this incident was merely that, an incident. I think the relationship was still new and exciting, and this was a small bump in the road.

Mike was a man's man. He was a former football player from the local high school. He was a strong fella working in hard-labor jobs. Some who knew him from high school thought he was a bit of a jerk, a "Mr. Tough Guy" of sorts, but others saw him as a nice, quiet guy. Sometimes quiet, physically fit guys get that stereotype of being a hard-ass, but I think most who knew Mike didn't see him that way.

When asked the question, "Could Mike have committed this crime?" most who knew him said, in their heart, "No," but do we really know what people are capable of? I am an acquaintance of Mike's, but I don't know him personally. I don't know what type of guy he really is. I know when we have run into each other, he has always been very cordial and pleasant to talk to, but can I tell if he could do something like murder? No. To me it seems unlikely. From what I know of him from others, he ] doesn't seem to be the type that could do this, especially if it was an accident, then go on with his life without having emotional troubles. Again, I don't know him well, but I think it would have eaten him alive. I think he would have spoken to someone or would have had severe issues with coping. Do my deductions make him innocent? Absolutely not. Could someone like Mike do this and not let anyone know or be able to hide it for this long? Unfortunately, yes. It has happened before.

In season five of the *Unraveled* podcast, hosted by long time true crime writer Billy Jensen and true crime podcaster Alexis Linkletter, they spend a whole season looking at individuals that executed the most heinous crimes imaginable but never perpetrated another crime like that in their lives. These individuals went decades without being detected, and they all got away with it because they didn't tell anyone. They went on to lead normal lives. They fit into their environments like everyone else but were able to hide that deep, dark secret.

Mike went on to get married, have children, and work a stable job for a very long time. Like many people, he did get a divorce but never has had a problem with the law or been in trouble. Could he have done it? Yes. Is it likely? I don't think so. Can he be completely cleared until this case is solved? No. There are still some unanswered questions about Mike, but unless he answers them, or evidence links him to her case, we will never know for sure.

Some things that keep Mike as a person of interest in my opinion are:

As a twenty-something attractive young male who gets a phone call from his twenty-three-year-old, beautiful girlfriend who says she is coming over, how could you fall asleep? I was married at twenty-three, and my wife is going to be really mad at me for saying this, but if she even looked at me a certain way, I wasn't going to sleep, if you know what I mean. It seems odd that he would do that in his situation.

If Laney didn't show up, why was he not concerned until the morning before he went to work? Again, I don't know if maybe he did have concerns and thought, *Well, she is an adult, and maybe she changed her mind.* Actually, as stated before, Laney was known to tell friends she was headed one place, then randomly show up somewhere else. Maybe she had done that with Mike at some point previously. The relationship was new, and Laney had no obligation to show up there even after he claimed she said she was coming over.

Rumor has it that Mike knew about Laney going to Gilmore Lanes to play pool, but he didn't show up. Why? Supposedly he had a long day at work and had to rest because he had to get up the next morning for another hard day. Could this be true? Absolutely. It was a Tuesday night. Not exactly the best night to go out and drink. Being out late or hungover the next morning could make work a bit difficult. Could he have shown up and seen something he didn't like between Laney and Shad? Maybe. Could he have been in the parking lot or frustrated at home and she did actually arrive there? Possibly. We will never know if this occurred, unless Mike comes forward with that information.

The last thing that keeps Mike in the crosshairs is that his alibi cannot be confirmed. No one in his house can say for sure if Laney ever came to the house or if Mike left at any point. We know that family bonds are very strong. Could the family be keeping information from the police to protect Mike? Yes. But again, we may never know this unless someone slips or their conscience gets the best of them one day.

The one thing that is on Mike's side is he wasn't at the bowling alley that night. Unfortunately for him, he will always be connected by a phone message linking his home to the last known location

Laney was supposed to arrive at. The darkness still hides the thirty minutes of the timeline between leaving the bowling alley in route to Mike's house and her death.

So who else was close enough to Laney to be on the radar of the investigation? Who would possibly have a grudge or be so vigorously jealous that physical violence could be the end result of a drunken encounter? Earlier I spoke of victimology. What relationships did Laney have in her past that could lead to murder?

Laney was gorgeous, and attention was nothing new for her, but oftentimes when searching for companionship her emotions were blind to the character of some of those individuals she tended to gravitate toward. She had a steady boyfriend in high school who, from all accounts I have heard, was a really good guy. He truly treated her well, but like most high school relationships, they grew apart as life took them in different directions. Laney seemed to be the type of person who loved independence but also may have been afraid to be alone. This caused her to look in many different directions for love. Like many young women, she longed for excitement and adventure, sometimes going after that proverbial "Bad Boy"— the guy slightly on edge who pushes the limits. The guy that many say you don't want to take home to your parents. Enter Matthew.

Exactly how Laney and Matthew got together is still foggy. I'm not really sure where or how they met, but if you were to look at the pictures of each of them separately, I would say it didn't seem like a match. I know I am judging a book by its cover, and I have never met either of them, but I think most would say this was not what you would expect as a happy couple. Matthew was described to me as a scammer, taking advantage of anyone he could to make a buck. He seemed to be allergic to finding real work and resorted to making money in questionable ways. Somehow Matthew was able to talk Laney into moving into an apartment with him in Fairfield. This started a tumultuous string of serious confrontations between him and Laney. Their fights were described as violent and out of control. Screaming turned to physical abuse. Arguments turned to knock-down, drag-out wars that could last for hours or even days.

Matthew seemed to me to be the wannabe tough guy but didn't realize Laney wasn't taking that shit! After speaking with Brittany, a friend of Laney's who lived above her in those apartments, I got the picture that this relationship was really starting to take its toll on Laney. She was tired, mad, frustrated, and just plain scared toward the end of their time together. When asking her friends to describe Laney to me, both physically and emotionally, almost all of them spoke about an actual scar. This scar was deep and the result of a knife fight between Matthew and Laney. It was time to get out. With the help of Brittany, other friends, and her family, Laney was able to break up with Matthew and move out, getting away from the day-to-day trauma of that relationship. Unfortunately, getting completely away would take more time. Time that Laney did not have.

Do these relationship issues make Matthew a killer? Maybe.

Would his violent nature have taken over and caused him to stalk Laney until the opportunity was right? Possibly.

Was he in the area when Laney walked out that door and into the darkness? We don't know.

The reasons for looking into Matthew seem to be obvious. He had a violent nature, and physical altercations between him and Laney were common. Matthew even demonstrated he had the ability to be violent with his own mother. Through our research, we did find another possible reason for Matthew to be extremely upset with Laney. About three months prior to that fateful night, he and Laney had to go to court for a default of some sort. Not exactly sure what the case was about, but the court decided Laney was not responsible and Matthew was. She was dropped from the case, but he had to pay a pretty hefty fine. There was another situation we uncovered. Laney had made her break from Matthew about a year prior, but during the separation, Laney may have grabbed a few things that belonged to Matthew that he would later want back. Did she do this to piss him off? From what I have learned about her, I would say yeah, probably. A week or two before her death, Laney and EJ got together to sit around a bonfire. The bonfire needed a bit of fuel to get started, so Laney offered to help. She happened to have a plastic-covered, detachable boat cushion that could be used as kindling for a fire. I think you know where I'm going with this.

Did she do this to get back at Matthew? Absolutely!

Did this spark his anger to get back at her? Possibly.

The questionable things about Matthew as a person of interest is that he would have had to know exactly where Laney was that night. He would have had to somehow coerce her outside, which from what her friends say about their relationship would have been very unlikely. If he didn't have contact with her prior to her going to the alley, then he would have had to stalk her or be in the right place at the wrong time. We do know he had a boat with a missing cushion, so could he know where to take her and her car into the river? Yes, he most likely knew a great deal about the local waters. Would he be able to accomplish the feat of subduing Laney, getting her body to the water, then getting rid of her car? From all the research we have done on him and from his stature, build, and intelligence, I really don't think so. He would have needed help, but maybe he did have others in his weird world of debauchery that would have helped him. An issue with that scenario is that it would be very difficult for the people around Matthew to never slip up and say something. Also, from what I have learned about Matthew, I believe one of his counterparts would have definitely thrown him under the bus for the $15K reward that was being offered for information leading to the arrest of a culprit in Laney's death. Can

Matthew be ruled out as a person of interest? No, he cannot. Until he can, we have to keep him on the radar.

I've mentioned several times in this chapter Laney's "love of her life," EJ. Surely, the love of her life couldn't do this, right? He wouldn't kill her accidentally, then try to cover it up, would he? Unfortunately, we don't know enough about EJ to determine his capabilities. Does he have to stay in our view as a person of interest? I think he has to be in the lens until we can completely eliminate him. EJ was an avid boater on the Ohio River near Manchester. Manchester is approximately two hours from Fairfield and sits right on the Ohio River. Would he have had easy access to the river to place Laney and her car there? Yes.

EJ's family was well known in town, owning a great deal of land. His uncle was a member of the Ohio House of Representatives. It has been expressed to me by a mutual acquaintance of EJ's that his uncle's reputation may have been used to get EJ out of some trouble with the law on a few occasions. This has not been confirmed, but did he feel he was above the law? Maybe.

EJ was also a part of the rodeo crowd. As a matter of fact, this was how Laney and her friends got started on the rodeo tour. Again, through my friend in the rodeo business, I was able to get a little information about EJ. Like Shad, EJ was a bull and bronc rider. His potential may have been a little better than that of Shad's, but still his chances of making it big weren't exactly high. What EJ had going for him were his looks and demeanor. He was a built young man with a captivating smile. He and Laney seemed to be the perfect rodeo couple in their cowboy boots and hats strutting around the rodeo grounds like *Yellowstone*'s Rip and Beth. The relationship was hot, and it seemed to be destiny for them to find each other.

EJ and Laney met at the Cheyenne Cattle Company Saloon and line-dancing venue. I can imagine it was kind of like those movie encounters in which EJ sees Laney on the dance floor in her tight Wrangler jeans and white cowboy hat. He can't take his eyes off her, when she suddenly turns around and makes eye contact. They gravitate to each other, and the screen starts to fade as they embrace. Okay, that's a bit mushy, but you get what I mean. Rip, the rugged bad-boy cowboy, and Beth, the beautiful, tough cowgirl, riding off into the sunset. As we know, real-life love stories don't always go as planned.

EJ was a bit of a ladies' man. Attractive, muscular, rowdy, and loved to have fun. Laney was searching for more. Marriage and children were becoming a major objective of her life. This may have brought up some emotions leading to frequent and sometimes physical fights between them. My friend in the rodeo world told me about a time when Laney and EJ were fighting at a rodeo and he had to go over and stop EJ from choking Laney. According to him, the fight was loud and violent. He feared EJ may hurt Laney so he and some other cowboys went over to break them up. Was this type of fight normal? We don't know, but her friends said it wasn't completely unusual. I don't think these confrontations were anything like those between Laney and Matthew, but they were physical. The friends seem to think the reason for the fights and eventual breakup was Laney's overbearing desire to get married and have kids and EJ's extreme aversion to both of those. Does this make EJ a killer? I don't know. Does it seem likely? Not really.

Questions that need to be answered to eliminate EJ are as follows:

Where was he that night? We know that he wasn't inside the bar, but we don't know where he was after she left. In one of his interviews, he stated he was either in Chicago, where he lived for a while, or at his home near Manchester.

EJ said in an interview that he spoke with Laney on the phone the morning of her disappearance. If they were not dating and she was with someone else, why were they talking on the phone that morning? Also, he would have known where she was going if they had spoken that day.

He mentioned he felt they would one day get back together. Did he see her dating someone new as a threat and wanted to discuss that in person? Did they meet outside that alley or somewhere else and things got out of hand? As mentioned earlier, Laney would often drop everything to go meet EJ. Did she do that this night?

A witness mentioned to us that Laney kept going to the door as if she was looking for someone to arrive. Was that Mike, or could it have been EJ?

Do any of the above scenarios seem likely? Not really. But as I have learned from several of my law enforcement connections, there cannot be any stone unturned. The leads, however unlikely, have to be eliminated. Were these leads looked into by the police agencies who were working on Laney's case? Yes, but I don't think complete answers were ever found to completely rule EJ out as a person of interest—or Mike or Matthew, for that matter.

Previously, I spoke of the many people in the bar that night with secrets to hide. Some hiding more than others, but each one unique. A used car sales manager with a violent past with women. A person arrested for impersonating a law officer and kidnapping. One individual with violent outbursts with a court date the next day. Another with a possible alcohol problem who may have been in the wrong place at the wrong time. Rumors of police involvement started to surface back then, and still today suspicions run wild. Convicted killers were interviewed in prison while a neighbor with connections to the alley had a strange story to tell a friend. The unfortunate part of that particular night was the number of wolves hiding in plain sight, waiting for the opportunity to take down their unsuspecting prey. Perhaps on any other night in that bowling alley, the chances of that many people with violent secrets went way down.

The crazy thing about all of these individuals was they all had a connection to the rivers in the area. Was there link to the river significant enough to consider them all as persons of interest, or am I creating that connection because I want them to be linked? That is something hard to figure out because the river is so important to this case. Am I fitting the relationship of these individuals to the river because it fits the narrative, or is it truly an important aspect of the case? I would say a little bit of both. I hope to show the unbiased importance as we continue to discuss these people, but it is hard not to want to make things fit together neatly.

As Evan and I dug through the mounds of information we were gathering, a friend of Laney's told the local Fox News station about what we were doing. Reporter Jessica Schmidt had just aired a story about Laney's case on her special segment of the news called "The Crime Vault." Jessica contacted me to see if we were interested in doing a story on the news about the work Evan and I were doing. I was a bit hesitant to do this because we aren't experts in investigations. I didn't want people to get the wrong impression about the purpose of our work. But Jessica convinced me it would be a great way to bring awareness back to Laney's case. Who knows? Maybe if someone hears the story about a student and a teacher trying to make a difference in Laney's case, they may come forward to the police with information.

At the time, her unsolved murder was going on two decades with little to no movement. Her family and friends were getting frustrated with what seemed to be a lack of progress by the departments working on the case. Laney's mother and father had passed away without answers to who may have killed their only daughter. When talking with David, Laney's only brother, and her friends, the emotions were still burning deep.

We agreed to do the interview. We asked Jessica to make sure to focus on our goal of keeping Laney's story alive. The case had gone cold, and it was falling into those dusty old file boxes in a dark, damp back room of the police department. We wanted to reach out to people who may have some information to help dust those boxes off.

Shortly after the story was aired, we began to get some help from people who saw the story. We were hoping that people with information would take it to the police, but what happened is they began to email me or call me to talk about what they thought could help. This is not what we were expecting, but I think many of the people who contacted us didn't want to take information to the police because they didn't know if it was important enough. Talking to police officers can be intimidating. Believe me, I know from this experience. I think they felt it would be easier to talk to us.

Some said they had been there that night, others had heard rumors, and some just wanted to stick their nose in it. After talking with my retired detective friends, I found out this is exactly what happens to them during a case.

One of the first to contact us was a man by the name of Mike Sturgeon. Mike is an extremely nice individual with his heart in the right place. When he saw the story, he told me he had to speak with me because of a conversation he had with a fellow car salesman that had continued to creep him out ever since it took place. Mike was a bit apprehensive at first because he felt that maybe he was betraying his colleague who had opened up to him in confidence.

Mike had been in the car business for quite a long time and had seen his share of good and not-so-good people working in the industry. As he contemplated calling me, he said his daughters were his inspiration to do what he felt was the right thing. "I have daughters, and I cannot imagine the pain. My heart goes out to her family and all of those who have poured their hearts into her case."

Mike had to get this information off his chest even if it didn't amount to anything.

He told me the story of a time a 1990s black Honda Del Sol pulled into the car lot, when out of the blue a coworker, let's call him Eddie, began to talk of bad memories regarding a black Honda Del Sol. Eddie began speaking of "that girl" from the bowling alley back in 1997. Mike remembered how Eddie described her as "extremely pretty" and how he knew her before that night. Eddie told Mike he was there that night and can still remember how she looked. He went on to talk about speaking with her in the bar and that Laney didn't really want to talk to him much. Mike could not remember all of the details, but he remembered him speaking of the car and how it was most likely in the river somewhere and the police would probably never find it. Mike told me he seemed to know a lot of details about the night and that Eddie almost seemed to go into a bit of trance while talking about Laney. Mike became uncomfortable with the conversation because Eddie seemed overly concerned about being at the bar that night. He tried to change the conversation because it began to make his "skin crawl," but Eddie continued his story. After the awkward moment was over, they went on their ways, never to speak about it again.

The years passed, and Eddie and Mike went in different directions with their jobs, keeping in touch sparingly. Mike didn't think about that conversation for nearly twenty years until he saw the FOX19 News report with Laney's picture on the screen. The story rushed back to him. He felt he had to pass on that information to someone, so he called me.

When I first talked with Mike, I wasn't sure if this information would be of any help. Was this someone who wanted to be a part of something to get some attention or did this conversation really happen? Evan and I had to try to figure out if this was an actual lead. But first we had to figure out who Eddie was.

Was he really at the bowling alley that night?

Did he really know Laney before that night?

Was Eddie merely a big talker and wanted attention?

Would Eddie have had the ability to get close enough to Laney that night?

Would he have had the ability to commit this type of crime?

Would he have been able to keep it a secret, other than telling Mike, for all these years?

We dug deep into Eddie's life. We found out through Laney's friends that even though her 1993 black Honda Del Sol was her pride and joy, her new country-western craze led her to begin looking for a truck. She liked the idea of being the tough cowgirl driving a pickup truck. One of her friends said that Laney had been looking at a truck at the Honda dealer where she'd bought her car. It so happens that Honda dealer was and still is almost directly across the street from the bowling alley. We had to find out if Eddie worked at that dealership. We confirmed that the car salesman from dealerships surrounding the alley would often finish their night at the bar at Gilmore Lanes. If this was true and Eddie worked at that dealership, then it would be plausible for him to have been there on the night of December 9th. I reached out to the dealership to see if they could give me any information of Eddie's employment during 1997 or 1998. They informed me that information is confidential and they would not be able to release that to me without a subpoena from a court of law. I completely understood their position as personnel information is protected, but I wasn't going to give up that easily.

It's good to have friends in high places like my friend Jamie. Shortly out of high school, Jamie began working at the Toyota dealership right next door to Honda. Actually, the dealerships were owned by the same group of people. I knew he most likely didn't know Eddie, but he was pretty well connected to some of the higher-ups in that area. I asked him if he happened to remember who the general manager of the Honda dealer was back in 1997. Jamie's memory was tremendous, and he gave me the name of that manager without hesitation. The only issue now was to find him. Evan's keen cyber-research methods found him within a day or two. Lucky for us, the general manager was still in the business. He'd moved to Columbus to run a dealership there. We connected with him and he seemed certain Eddie did work at that Honda dealer from the mid-1990s to around 1999. Could Eddie have been at the alley that night? Yes, he most definitely could have been.

Mike continued to describe Eddie to me over the next few months. He stated that Eddie wasn't a very good person, especially when it came to women. He was vulgar, hateful, and aggressive. Eddie was known to brag about the women he slept with and how badly he treated them. Eddie was very experienced with the court system. He had been in front of a judge for theft, drugs, alcohol, foreclosure, tax evasion, and domestic violence. As we looked carefully into his background on the Hamilton County Clerk of Courts records, we could see all of his prior encounters with the law, but the domestic violence charges caught our eye. Although domestic violence is repugnant, one incident could have been the result of a bad argument that may have gotten out of control, but three times is a pattern. Eddie was violent to women, and that's not okay. As a matter of fact, two of those charges happened in 1997, the year Laney went missing. Just seven months, almost to the date, prior to that fateful night, Eddie was in jail for "Domestic Violence – Knowingly," according to the Hamilton County Clerk of Courts records.

Eddie had hit our radar early in our research, but we didn't realize it until Mike came forward. If you remember the introduction to this book, I mentioned a gentleman at the bowling alley who asked if we needed help. He became a good source of information about the bowling alley and the people there because he had been bowling and working there for nearly forty years. In our initial conversation, he mentioned he was at the alley that night. He remembers leaving the alley around ten or ten thirty p.m. On his way out, he stated he had seen Laney outside smoking and talking with a gentleman in a dress shirt and tie. Was this Eddie? We cannot confirm that information. The description our source gave us was a younger, business-like type of man. He even mentioned the male figure looked and dressed like the car salesmen who came to the bar to drink after work. He stated he was average size with short hair.

Unfortunately, our witness was fighting cancer at the time of our discussions. Shortly into our relationship with this individual, he passed. We were not able to show him a six-pack with Eddie's picture in it before he became too sick. Now, this by no means proves Eddie was there or was the guy Laney was speaking with, but it did give us some things to look into as we moved forward.

Another witness in an interview with police in 1998 mentioned a similar story. This person was also a bowler that night. He told a friend that he saw Laney leave with a car salesman but later told the police it was another girl that was there that night. The only problem with the second part of his story is that every other witness there that night only remembers Laney, because you couldn't miss her. Who was this other girl and could you really mix her up with Laney?

Eddie fit the description of average size, at about 165 pounds, short hair, wearing a dress shirt and tie, and the fact was that he was a car salesman, but we still haven't confirmed he was even there. Mike's creepy conversation was merely that. A creepy conversation. But it got even more creepy when I was looking through some information I had received about the case.

Early in the year of 1998, a man named Greg called the Union

Township police to relay a message about a conversation he'd heard at a bar in which Eddie, the service/used car manager of the Honda dealer, was talking about the girl who disappeared. Greg overheard Eddie talking to someone about how he and his friends were at the bowling alley that night. Eddie stated he and his friends often went to Gilmore Lanes to unwind after work. The part of Greg's message to the police that really made us believe Eddie could be a viable person of interest is that he felt as if Eddie seemed "overly concerned" about the missing young lady. These were the exact same words used by Mike nearly twenty years later. There is something about Eddie's story that evokes emotions in people they don't normally feel.

Could Eddie be telling anyone that will listen that he knows something?

Is he somehow either reliving what happened or trying to ask for help?

Could Eddie be the guy in the dress shirt and tie seen talking with Laney outside?

Did she reject an advancement by Eddie and he snapped? We know from his record that someone seven short months earlier saw his violent nature.

As we continued to dig deep into Eddie's life, we found that his residence at the time of Laney's disappearance was in an area with very close access to the Great Miami River in a spot that we had marked as a possible place for someone to try to dispose of her or the car. Mike had also told us that Eddie would often brag about the times he and his rowdy friends would spend wild, drunken nights on a boat on the Ohio River. We were able to confirm through records obtained in a FOIA request that Eddie was at the bowling alley bar on December 9, 1997. Does any of the information prove Eddie committed this horrendous act? No, it does not. Does it lead us to believe he could have done it? Yes, I think so, but there are others that still need to be looked into before we make any inferences about the most logical perpetrator to this crime.

The goal for Laney that night was to take a deep breath after long semester of classes. Hang out with friends, drink, play some pool, and simply be twenty-three. It didn't exactly work out like she had planned, but that didn't keep her from enjoying her night at the bar with a friend. The choice to go to the Gilmore Bowling Lanes bar was for the cheap beer and the pool tables. Drinking, playing pool, and showing off were some of Laney's favorite things to do.

While playing pool, there were some people with similar pastimes in the corner of the bar. A group that we coined the "Group of Six" was sitting in the corner of the small bar doing their best to figuratively keep up with Laney and Shad in the drinking department. The "Group of Six" consisted of five males and one female. The five males were obviously aware of Laney being in the room, while the young female was doing her best to make sure that one of them, her boyfriend, wasn't noticing too much. Three of them seemed to get over the rubbernecking as she walked by fairly quickly, while two of them may have paid a bit more attention most of the night. The group was having some fun in the corner mostly by themselves, but the female of the group and her boyfriend did put their quarters down on the pool table to call next when the previous game was over.

Noticing that Laney and Shad seemed to be together, possibly as a couple, they offered to play with them for a game or two. The young lady was impressed with Laney, not only with her looks, but also with the way she handled herself. But after the game, they went their own ways to continue the party. Although they tried not to look too much, the "Group of Six" found it hard not to notice every time Laney would go to the bar.

One of the males, let's call him Wayne, was extremely interested in Laney's presence. Wayne was a large man. His stature may have been considered a bit intimidating by some, but his attitude was what seemed to be the problem. According to the young woman in the group, Wayne was a bit of a ladies' man, or at least he thought he was. He spent a great deal of the night leering at Laney so much that the bowling alley owner told the police there was a tall stranger at the bar who seemed extremely interested in her as she would approach the bar. In our research, it came up that the bartender actually stated, "A weird, tall guy had been staring at her all night."

The owner of the alley was so concerned about him that he did his own checking around to see who this man was after the police spoke to him. He knew one member of the "Group of Six," who happened to be a bowler in the leagues, and asked if he knew the man. It was told to him that his name was Wayne. Once we found this bit of information, we had to dig deep to see who Wayne and the rest of the "Group of Six" were.

Were the "Group of Six" great friends or only acquaintances?

Were the "Group of Six" normal, law-abiding citizens just having a good time?

Was anyone in the "Group of Six" hiding some type of secret?

Was it normal for Wayne to stare at females this way?

What did each of the six see that night?

We began to look carefully at each of the backgrounds of the "Group of Six." As we scoured through documents, court records, and social media pages, it was hard to find a true picture of each person in the group, especially how they were back in 1997. Nothing special seemed to stick out about most of them. Minor traffic incidents, financial issues, minor drug possession, and divorces seemed to be the only things we could find. At a glance, these individuals probably wouldn't have been considered a threat to anyone, and murder didn't seem possible.

We continued to plow through information until a few things

caught our eye. We stumbled upon a few encounters Wayne had with the law. Wayne was a bit of a troublemaker in his youth. Like the others, he had a few minor traffic and possession issues, but he also had some more serious problems. Some of these run-ins with the law included weapons and a shattered windshield after a night of drinking. Just because he did some pretty stupid things, it doesn't necessarily make him a person of interest in Laney's murder, but it was intriguing to look at his past. It appeared that Wayne was somewhat of a hothead. His emotions often got him into troubled waters. His actions included carrying a concealed weapon, shooting into a crowd at a festival, pulling a knife on a man he had a disagreement with, and busting the windshield and side mirror of a female's car outside of bar in Fairfield. It would appear that during his early twenties, Wayne may have had anger issues. The interesting part about these legal issues was that many of them occurred only a few short months before December 9, 1997.

Was Wayne having a breakdown?

Was the world caving in on him and he was on the verge of snapping?

These are questions that only could be answered by talking with Wayne, but due to the fact that this is still an open case, I don't want to step on any toes or get in the way by confronting him directly. As the years pass in the case, I'm not sure how long I will be able to resist the urge to speak with him. For now, we will keep searching for more information.

What we were able to do was talk about Wayne with the young lady that was a part of the "Group of Six." The surprising thing about her is that she has only been interviewed once by authorities since 1997. The first time she was ever spoken to was in 2005, eight years after Laney's disappearance. The questioning was slightly vague and seemed to be more of a protocol interview than an actually credible witness interview. Her answers seemed evasive and, to me, it sounded as if she was scared to implicate herself or anyone in the group.

Until we contacted her, no one had spoken to her since that 2005 interview. In twenty-five years, stories change, people change, relationships change, but one thing that does not change is the fact that Laney is gone. For this woman, who is in her late forties now, it has been buried in her conscience all this time and, according to her, each day it goes unsolved the memories of that night haunt her. She has wondered for years if she missed anything that could be important to the case.

Who else did she see that night who may have stood out?

Could she remember any interactions that appeared uncomfortable between Laney and a possible person of interest?

Could someone from the "Group of Six" have been involved?

Mark, my retired detective friend, spoke with her at length over the phone, asking questions about that night, trying to put her back in the bar. If she could go back in time to sit at that corner table, as an underage drinker, hiding from the police, could she focus enough to remember anything? "Laney was already in the bar when I arrived shortly after ten p.m.…. Of course, all the guys in the bar, including the guys in my group, had made comments about the girl in the tight Wrangler jeans," she quipped.

As Mark continued to ask her questions, he began to focus on the individuals from her group. She went on to tell him that she really only knew her boyfriend, who later became her husband, Wayne, and another guy, but the name seemed to slip her mind at the time.

As she continued to talk about that night, events seemed to be coming back to her memory. Understandably, if an event didn't really affect you in the long run, details start to fade, and sometimes when asked about that night, your mind will fill in the gaps the way you want them to come out. Was she fitting her memory to the story or was she really remembering things that truly happened? Unfortunately, this is extremely hard to determine. But we also know that in interviews there will most likely be some truth that shines through.

In that first discussion with Mark, she mentioned Wayne was the only one to interact with Laney, other than playing pool. This statement was just her recollection of that night, but let's say I'm pretty sure that night was a bit of a blur for her, so we may never know if it is completely true. There may have been an offer to buy her a drink or a conversation with a proposition of some sort. She said Wayne came away from the interaction with frustration. He was irritated by the rejection of the girl everyone was enamored with that evening. She recalled that Wayne actually left the bowling alley for a period of time. She could not remember how long he was gone or what time it was, but she said the only reason she remembers this detail was because he left the building with a flannel, zip-up, hoodie-type shirt, then returned to the bar with just a white T-shirt. On the front of the T-shirt appeared to be some specks or stains that could have been vomit. She stated the shirt was wet and Wayne's frustration seemed pretty strong at this point. Mark asked if she recalled seeing Laney at that point, and she stated she didn't remember seeing her at that time. The girl everyone had been watching suddenly was not noticed. Could she have gone to the restroom? Could she have been out in the alley? Could she have stepped outside for a smoke? Yes, to all of these, but it does make one wonder where Laney might have been at that time.

The point that caught our attention most was the fact Wayne had left for a period of time, possibly when Laney was not in the bar either. In an interview on December 15, 1997, Wayne admitted to being outside by himself. He stated to authorities he was sick and went outside to throw up. He stated he was so sick he threw up on himself, then proceeded to pass out in the back seat of his car. Later, our witness and her boyfriend allegedly went to the parking lot to leave and came upon Wayne lying in his car. Being the good friends they were, they decided to take Wayne home. The boyfriend drove Wayne's car while she followed in hers. When they arrived at Wayne's home, they gave him his keys and watched as he went inside. The couple drove off to their destination and did not hear from Wayne for several days.

The only communication from Wayne after that night was a phone call to ask them if they had heard about the girl at the bar going missing. When looking at the news outlets from that time period, it appears the story of her disappearance didn't reach the news until the weekend after her disappearance, and the first newspaper report didn't come out until December 13, 1997. Yet our witness believed he asked that question before the weekend. If the story had not come out yet, how did he know she was missing?

The strangest part about Wayne after Laney went missing was his apparent disappearance from the area and lack of communication with the friends who he spent most of his time with. His friends, concerned when he did not return phone calls, drove to the house where they dropped him off that night to check on him. What they found was a bit strange but didn't seem to be that big of a deal at the time. He was gone. Gone where? A person at the home told them he left town to go live with a relative out of state.

Why did he leave town?

Where did he go?

Why didn't he tell his friends he was leaving?

Why would he make this sudden change at that exact time?

The authorities did track Wayne down to get an interview, but since Laney was only missing when they interviewed him, he wasn't treated as a person of interest. He was simply a witness in the bar that night. He was questioned about that night over the phone while he was with his relative in Texas. That conversation took place on December 15, 1997, five days after her disappearance.

Now, he'd gone to Texas with no prior communication with anyone close to him.

Why then?

What was he running from?

Were the demons he was fighting too strong?

We needed to clear up some things that our witness had told Mark during the first interview. We set up a time to meet her at a local watering hole. One of the things I have learned from the retired detectives I have been working with is to make the witness feel comfortable. Find a location, like a local bar, to sit and have a drink while we talk about that night. After exchanging pleasantries, Mark went over the questions he asked her the first time to see if she was consistent with her answers.

Did you come to the alley by yourself or with someone?

Were you drinking? If so, what were you drinking?

What were you wearing?

These questions were asked to jog her memory about the setting in the bowling alley. Where was everyone? Who was there? Were there any other people that caught her attention? In our long discussion, Mark found her to be consistent with almost all the answers.

Then she began to talk about the encounters she and her group of six had with Laney. Most of them had very little interaction, other than the constant stares by the guys in the group. She noted that she may have played one game of pool with Laney and Shad, but the conversation was limited to small talk if they even spoke at all.

Then she surprised us with a comment about Wayne. She didn't think much of it back then, but she now remembered that Wayne had followed Laney to the bar several times. After one trip to the bar, she stated Wayne seemed irritated with Laney's dismissal of his advances. She quoted him as saying, "That bitch thinks she is too good for me!" As they had in the past, she and her boyfriend sloughed it off with a laugh as if him getting rejected was nothing new. She even stated she saw Laney in the ladies' room and apologized for Wayne's annoying behavior. We don't know if this interaction really happened. Could our witness be unintentionally telling us something that did not happen because she felt we needed a specific answer? Yes.

It had been twenty-five, almost twenty-six years at this time. She was only spoken to once about that night in 2005, until we reached out. She expressed to us how she truly wanted to help get answers for this crime, because it had been with her all these years. "I have been upset all this time because I didn't pay more attention that night," she stated. Could her brain be creating something to give us the answers she thinks we want to hear? Possibly. But she was consistent with describing the interactions between Wayne and Laney. The bowling alley owner corroborated her observation in his "strange, tall man" statement in his interview with the police. In light of how the evening ended, whether this information is exactly correct or not, we have to take her seriously. We have to continue to search for other individuals who may have seen or heard similar things that night. We are currently trying to connect with the rest of the "Group of Six" to get their memories of the night that has to be stuck in their minds forever.

Is Wayne a killer? We don't know. Did his actions before, during, and after that infamous night at the bowling alley put him under the microscope as a person of interest? Yes, I don't think we can deny he needs to be looked into as a strong candidate for the perpetrator. He was supposedly sick outside of the bowling alley for a period of time. Unfortunately, the members of the "Group of Six," including himself, didn't know exactly when during the night this occurred or the duration of time he was alone. His shirt was wet sometime during that night, according to our witness and her boyfriend, and he had shed his hoodie. He had previous acts of anger in social situations. He was an avid fisherman, who knew a great deal about the best places to fish in the area. The home his friends possibly took him to at the end of the night was very close to the Great Miami River, near a location where a witness expressed they may have seen a black sports car and a truck pull onto a gravel road that leads to the river. Through the information gathered in the FOIA request and from our witness from the Group of Six, Wayne unexpectedly left town to live in Texas shortly after Laney's disappearance. Texas is where that December 15, 1997, interview mentioned earlier took place. Through our efforts to track Wayne down, we were able to find he had gotten married in Texas and lived there for two years before returning to the area.

Wayne was not the only one that night with a shady background and questionable circumstances. There were many people we have found with issues that could be considered problematic, but these, most likely, were about being suspiciously in the wrong place at the right time. Take, for instance, Sam, another member of the "Group of Six." Sam was the lesser-known acquaintance of the group. He knew most of the others in the group individually but didn't seem to be attached to any of them in a deeper friendship. The others that night spoke of just meeting him or being familiar with him through mutual connections. He came to the bar alone and was witnessed leaving alone around one or one thirty a.m.

Those who knew him better than the rest stated Sam was a hard worker, and he seemed very tired from the long workday. One of the friends mentioned that Sam left early because he had to go to work early the next morning. He specified Sam had not had much to drink that evening and seemed fine to drive home. These statements were most likely what the Fairfield PD considered a little strange. In Sam's interview five days after Laney's disappearance, he stated that he left the bar around two a.m. with two other members of the group, which did not match statements of the others. Sam also mentioned he had been "really drunk" and decided to drive to a local apartment complex to sleep off the buzz before heading home. He already had a DUI on record, so apparently out of fear, he decided not to take the chance of getting pulled over. This sounds like a very noble gesture of doing the right thing in the midst of a night of bad decisions.

Why did his friends say he was barely drinking when he said he was too drunk to drive home?

The next question arose quickly after his description of where he went to sleep it off. Sam gave a specific name of the apartment complex with the exact street he parked his car to fall asleep. He then went on to say that he arrived home in Hamilton, Ohio, at approximately five a.m.

If he was that drunk, how did he remember that specific location after he left the bar?

How did he spend close to two hours in his car trying to sleep off the beer goggles in temperatures close to forty degrees Fahrenheit?

The next question I would have asked him was why he drove approximately one mile south to that particular apartment complex if he lived nearly eight miles north? Most logical people will try to drive in the direction of their final destination, yet he went the opposite way. His landlord (and one-time band manager) gave a statement that he received a call from Sam around one thirty or two a.m., but he did not answer it. Sam left a message on a recorder saying he needed a ride home, and the landlord tried to call the number back, but the phone did not receive calls. That makes us believe it was from the payphone at the bowling alley. Not knowing where Sam was calling from, the landlord went to bed. When he arose for work the next morning, he stated Sam was there but didn't know if his car was there. From what I gather, Sam actually rented a room or a floor in the same house as the landlord. This explains how he would know if Sam had gone to work or if his car was near the house. He did state that Sam had gotten to work that day without asking for a ride, which he may have done before, so maybe his car made it home. The fact he called for a ride fit his "I'm too drunk" story, but was he claiming to be too drunk to drive because he needed help with something else? The landlord also stated in his interview with police that Sam told him he was questioned about Laney's disappearance and was concerned that the police would not believe his "sleeping off his buzz" story. Sam had some more explaining to do.

Why did he drive south instead of north?

Why did he drive a mile away, when there were two apartment complexes behind the alley, 0.1 and 0.2 miles away respectively?

Why didn't he stay in the bowling alley parking lot?

How did he withstand the cold for two to three hours in his car?

Why did he tell his landlord that he didn't think anybody would believe his story about parking at the apartments?

Sam's relationship to the river was simple. His address at the time of Laney's disappearance was a straight shot down the street, less than a mile from the Great Miami River, near the Columbia Bridge. This was very close to the dam we discussed in an earlier chapter. Sam was a long-time resident of the area, so his knowledge of the river was most likely pretty good. Does any of this prove that Sam is a killer? No.

Sam endured a great deal of scrutiny from the authorities over the years. He eventually decided that he no longer wanted to speak about this topic, so he hired a lawyer. In a statement to the sheriff's office, his lawyer informed them that Sam wished to invoke his right to remain silent. On Sam's behalf, he did cooperate with the authorities for quite some time before invoking this right. From information we have gathered about Sam after his ordeal over Laney's case, we know he struggled with this for years. Was Sam really a person capable of doing such an act of violence or was he simply in the wrong place at the right time?

Sam may have unfortunately been connected to something that would haunt him for life because of uncontrollable circumstances of being in that place on that night, but for Laney, it was exactly the wrong place at the wrong time. According to those who knew her best, this was the only time Laney had ever ventured into that particular bar, and sadly, it was also her last. As we looked deep into those close to her, acquainted with her, and those possible first-time encounters, we stumbled upon a very interesting character.

While talking with Angie, Laney's very close friend mentioned earlier in the book, she brought to our attention a name Detective Smith asked her about while looking into this case. Detective Smith was not as well versed in the technology of what was a somewhat new fad at the time, social media. He noticed Angie was good at finding information about people, so he thought he could use Angie's abilities to his advantage. She jumped in quickly, using Facebook and other new forms of social media to track this guy down. She even helped me find him on Facebook when I started looking into Laney's story. This man was definitely an interesting fella with a few skeletons in his closet. At first, it was difficult to find much on him, but if Detective Smith mentioned him, he must be important, so we kept digging.

One day, for a reason I have no idea, I began to look at local private investigators (PIs) in the area. I'm not sure if I was looking for help or taking a shot in the dark, but what happened was miraculous. I had never worked with a PI. I didn't even understand exactly what a PI was, but for some reason I thought it was a good idea. What we found gave me that eerie feeling someone or some-thing was directing me to do this from well beyond my Earthly reach.

While searching for a PI, a website suddenly jumped out at me. Unfortunately, it no longer exists, but it was called stilltheyspeak.-com. This website was designed by a victim of violent crime herself and a practicing PI. She was advocating to keep the stories relative of girls who were murdered in Kentucky and neighboring states. I immediately told Evan we needed to talk to her. We reached out several times, leaving voicemail messages and sending emails. It took a little time for her to get back with us.

Our initial communications were slightly frustrating as she informed us of her extremely busy schedule and her current venture to complete her doctoral thesis. We waited, impatiently, but we understood. Every once in a while, she would return a message about how she found some information on a particular man while she was looking into Laney's case. One thing she mentioned to us was that he lived in the apartment complex right across the street from the bowling alley. She recounted confronting this man with questions about that night at Gilmore Bowling Lanes. She wrote:

SEVERAL YEARS AGO, I IDENTIFIED SOMEONE WHO I BELIEVE IS responsible for her kidnapping and death. I located him and even went out to interview him and he did not deny it, rather seemed to enjoy it, and simply asked me where my evidence was that could prove it (he specifically stated DNA).

LIKE A GOOD INVESTIGATOR, SHE THEN SAID SHE COULDN'T divulge his name at that time because the case had still not been solved and she didn't want to compromise any investigation. In our discussion with Detective Smith, he had also mentioned he had gone to confront an individual, who had moved sometime after Laney's disappearance, in a small town in the nearby state of Indiana. The man refused to speak to him, emphatically saying, "You're that cold case guy, I'm not talking to you!" I'm pretty sure this was the same man, and that meant we had to keep digging.

Who was this mystery man?

How could we find out his name?

This individual appeared to be living close to the bowling alley when Laney went missing and then moved a few times. The PI and Detective Smith found him in Indiana around 2010, but where is he now?

Shortly after this email was sent, we found a resource in one of the local law enforcement entities that worked on Laney's case, willing to work with us. I will not at this time divulge that resource because he was trying to help us get Laney the attention her case deserved, and I don't want to cause him any grief. In his words, "These boxes have been sitting here for [twenty] years, someone should look at them." His extended experience arguing both the prosecution and defense side of the bench gave value to his professional opinion, which was that this case would not be solved until someone came forward and confessed. He felt that it might be okay to let us look at the case because it had been cold for way too long, and who knows, maybe, just maybe, we would find something.

Then one day, like those glowing pieces of evidence that show up within an hour in a *CSI* episode, there it was. The name of the man Angie had mentioned to me and the man the PI had been talking about. They were the same man. Now we had something to work with.

We jumped onto the Hamilton County and Butler County Clerk of Courts websites to do court records searches on the man. When we placed his name in the search window, up popped several cases. Many of them, however, were of another person with a similar name. Later we found the defendant of those cases turned out to be his son. Perfect example of the apple doesn't fall far from the tree.

One court entry really caught our attention from the municipal court records of the City of Fairfield, Ohio. In 1990, this man, let's call him KC, was arrested for kidnapping. We were able to request the records for this case to find the circumstances of this arrest. At a bar in Fairfield, a young woman was having some fun with friends when she decided to drunkenly flash KC inside the bar. KC decided this was his opportunity to take advantage of the situation. In his wallet was a gold shield of deception from his job as a security guard at a correctional institution in the area. He quickly flashed the shiny badge and told the young woman she was under arrest for indecent exposure. KC proceeded to falsely apprehend her and placed her in his car. In fear, the victim went along with the process. Her friends thought the actions of the police officer to be very strange. They followed them out to the car to find the car was not a real police car. KC expressed he was undercover and if they didn't get away from his car they would be arrested as well. They backed away as the car exited the parking lot.

Still uneasy with the situation, the friends waited long enough for the imposter to arrive at the police station, then called to verify their friend was there and to ask permission to come take her home. The answer they received was frightening. The police informed them they had no one in their precinct with the victim's name. In a panic, they informed the police of the frightening occurrence at the bar. The police seemed to respond with little surprise and informed the friends they were pretty sure where they needed to go. Within a few minutes, the police cruisers pulled into the apartment complex behind a car dealership that happened to sit adjacent to the Gilmore Bowling Lanes. When the police entered the apartment, they found the female victim lying on the living room floor with her hands cuffed behind her back. It appeared as if the police got there in time. She was not harmed. She was a bit shaken and still nursing a bit of a buzz. KC was arrested and taken to jail. He was charged with kidnapping. He would later have to appear in court, but like in many cases, the key piece to conviction is the testimony of the victim. She did not show up, and the charges were dropped to a misdemeanor with no jail time to be served.

This happened in 1990. Fast forward to the fall of 1997. KC was pulled over for a traffic violation at the intersection of Route 4 and South Gilmore Road. The exact intersection in front of the bowling alley where Laney was abducted. Again, this doesn't seem to be that big a deal, until we found the address reported on his driver's license. He still lived in that apartment right there by the alley.

In that same glimmering set of information that revealed KC, I also noticed a name from my past as kid growing up in Fairfield. Dr. Mark Godsey, a childhood friend of mine, now an extremely accomplished attorney and most impressively known for his tremendous work with the Ohio Innocence Project, was now a part of the list of people we needed to speak with. In a letter sent to the Butler County Sheriff's Office, Mark, with information found by the PI, wrote that KC was possibly a person of interest in the abduction and murder of Laney Gwinner.

Why would he be a person of interest in this case?

Why would Dr. Godsey think he needed to be looked into?

In 1991, a man by the name of Dean Gillispie was convicted of sexually assaulting three women on three different occasions in the Dayton, Ohio, area in 1988. The victims stated the man identified himself as a security guard, then proceeded to point a small silver gun at them. He told them to drive to a different location where he exposed himself, fondled their breasts, then forced them to perform oral sex on him. He then returned them to the spot from which he had abducted them and faded into the dark shadows of the night. The victims said the suspect wore sunglasses to hide his eyes. He called himself "Roger," a term often used by police, and felt it necessary to tell them he had been sexually assaulted by a relative when he was younger. The suspect was approximately 200-250 pounds, according to the victims, but they were not consistent on hair color and some other identifying features.

Unfortunately, for Dean this would be a long battle for him to win his freedom for a crime he did not commit. In Dr. Godsey's book *Blind Injustice,* you can read the tragic story of Dean's conviction, appeals, and eventual exoneration after twenty years in prison. You are probably wondering how KC and Laney had anything to do with Dean and his awful time spent in jail.

On that night in 1990, when KC used the fake police ruse to kidnap a victim, the real police officers allowed KC to keep his sunglasses on when they took his mugshot. Dr. Godsey and the PI noticed KC's arrest while looking into Dean's case. The use of the role of authority to kidnap a female seemed very similar to the cases in Dayton. The lack of certain physical actions against Laney as revealed by the autopsy may have fit the modus operandi of the Dayton perpetrator. During the time of the assaults in 1988, KC was employed by a local correctional institution that was approximately twenty to thirty minutes away from Dayton. Shortly before the 1988 incidents, he was arrested for DUI in close proximity to the abduction sites. KC is approximately 6'0" and 215 pounds, similar to the description given by the victims of those crimes. But the mugshot was what really did it. In his book, Dr. Godsey placed the artist rendition of the victims' descriptions of their attacker and KC's mugshot together, and the resemblance was staggering.

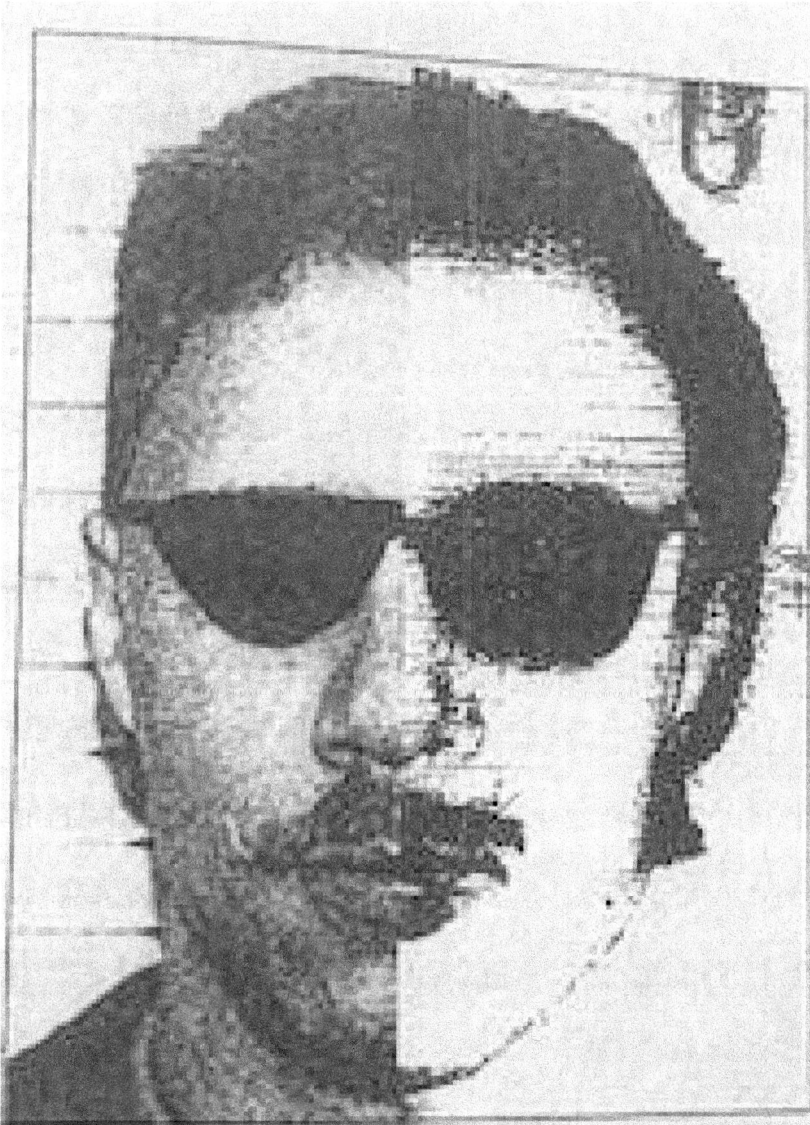

incriminating comments about the case when interviewed by DIP, after claiming to know nothing about Gillispie's "rape case," [ ] asked how the "victim" described the perpetrator, seemed obsessed with the case and whether police were re-opening it.

After discovering this information, we reached out to the PI to let her know we now knew the name of the man she had confronted. She then opened up a bit more about the process she went through to find and question KC. She did tell us about researching, then interviewing, the people at the bowling alley about what they remembered before, during, and after the night of December 9, 1997. Allegedly, witnesses described a man fitting KC's description. At least one person stated that he had seen a strange encounter between Laney and KC as she moved to the bar to get a drink. She didn't elaborate on what that interaction was, but it seemed to have garnered memorable attention from some of the patrons. It turned out KC had been to the alley many times before. He had been there enough for the witness and a couple of others to recognize him from a description the PI gave them. After they began to remember him, she presented them with a picture for them to confirm his identity. KC may have been there that night.

Shortly after that last conversation with the PI, she politely removed herself from our deep dive. She stated her time was needed elsewhere, but in reality I believe someone from the investigative team may have contacted her to ask her to stop speaking with us. Why? I'm not sure, but maybe they were afraid we were going to screw something up. Could there be other reasons? Maybe, but I won't speculate on that. Who knows? Maybe she truly didn't have time for us anymore, but she and Dr. Godsey gave us more questions to ask.

Was KC the actual perpetrator of the 1988 sexual assaults that sent an innocent man to prison for twenty years?

Was KC a serial rapist that almost got caught in 1990 in that apartment adjacent to the alley?

Did KC's uncontrollable urge to control someone take over on that dark, cold night of December 9, 1997?

Was there a fatal encounter in the parking lot that he has been hiding for nearly twenty-six years?

Is KC the wolf in sheep's clothing who revealed himself that night?

Unfortunately, Laney's case is the epitome of chasing the elusive lone wolf. There are so many directions this case can go, and, woefully, that is exactly what the police and our small group, which has grown from just Evan and me to now include a handful of retired detectives, has had to do. There doesn't seem to be a clear-cut direction to follow. Like in many true crime stories, there is no person to direct all the attention to. There is no ex-husband having an affair or in financial ruin who needs to get rid of his wife. There doesn't seem to be any particular family member who was jealous, mad, or unstable that would have capacity to kill Laney. Laney was beloved by her friends, so how could any of them be involved? She didn't live an extremely high-risk lifestyle, so the type of characters that delve into that world wouldn't be around to take Laney out.

The wolf is hiding in the woods, and we have to keep chasing it until we catch it. I truly believe our hunting dogs are on the scent of the murderous predator who took the life of an angel on Earth who God has given the wings of an angel in Heaven. Her presence is still felt today by those who loved her and by those of us trying to bring her justice. With the help of her and her heavenly family, we will find the wolf someday, but until then, we'll keep hunting.

# 8

# Uncovered in the Dark: The Profile of a Killer

**"The darkness uncovers the evils hidden in the light."**
— Randy Hubbard

THE ROOM IS FILLED with the haze of the dim lights of the bar. The hum of the neon Bud Light and Miller Light signs hanging on the wall create a continuous white noise. The crack of the cue ball breaking the rack becomes a normal part of the sounds of the night. The dull mumbling is broken by the sudden burst of laughter from the corner of the bar. A cheer from the pool table after a great shot quickly turns heads in that direction. The girl who drew that attention seems to be enjoying herself and in her element. After watching her for a second or maybe a little longer, things go back to normal. Friends talking over each other. Couples drinking quietly. The few loners who appear to be regulars sit by themselves at each end of the long bar. There is one old man sitting in the middle speaking to anyone who will sit close enough to him. Every once in a while, he throws out a funny one-liner when someone comes up to order a drink. Coworkers loudly lamenting the day stand close to the dart board. The smell of cheap beer and cigarette smoke swirls through the air each time the door opens where the fellas outside are finishing a quick smoke. The country music in the background from the jukebox will be stuck in the heads of the patrons for hours after. The famous sounds of Toby Keith, Shania Twain, or some Brooks and Dunn's "Boot Scootin' Boogie," interspersed with a sprinkling of Guns & Roses and Metallica, fills the room. The number of people in this small bar makes it feel a bit crowded, but everyone continues with the fun.

As the beer continues to flow, peoples' inhibitions start to fade. The guys who continue to look at Laney are gaining the confidence to try to see if they have the ability to catch her attention. Like male birds in the wild, the single guys, both young and old, begin to swell up a bit and start to find ways to get closer to her. One struts up to the pool table to lay some quarters down for the next game and the chance to watch her do her thing around the pool table. Another goes out of his way to accidentally bump into her on the way to the bar to get a drink. Even though many believe she is with the guy she came with, it now becomes a challenge. To some, it's a harmless game of cat-and-mouse for that quick moment of attention from the Wrangler jean model in the middle of the room. To others it becomes a much bigger and soon-to-be-darker provocation. In the dull, neon lights, evil is lurking, careful not to show itself.

Evil: "Let me buy you a drink, gorgeous."

Laney: "No, I'm good."

Evil: "I got the next one."

Laney: "No, really, I'm good."

The drinks are going down faster for the aggressive pursuer.

Caution is blowing into the wind with each drink, and now she's starting to become an obsession.

Evil: "Hey, babe, you wanna step outside?"

Laney: "What? No!"

Evil: "You know you want to!"

Laney: "Fuck off! Get away from me!"

Evil, whispering to himself: "Bitch!"

While this interaction was going on, the loner in the corner has been watching, as he has been all night. Deep stares through dark, hollow eyes. The urge within starts to take over, and before the night ends, he will have her. He contemplates when to take advantage of the situation. She has to leave sometime. He sits there hiding in plain sight until the time is right. Maybe she'll go to the restroom or out front to smoke. Maybe she'll gesture to her friend that she is about to leave. She's pretty drunk, so this could be easy for him, but the right time hasn't come yet. She seems to be making moves as if it's about time to go, moving closer to the door. Now is the time. As she moves into the darkness of the poorly lit parking lot, the evil wolf pounces.

What I'm doing here is what John Douglas, famous FBI profiler, talks about in his book *Journey Into the Darkness*. In the book, he walks the reader through the mind of a killer before, during, and after a horrendous murder. Mr. Douglas stated to a reporter, "This is what it means to walk in the shoes, to know both victim and subject—how each interacts with the other." He is trying to put himself in that scenario so he can figure out what type of person could commit such an act.

John Douglas is an expert in dealing with these awful human beings and the crimes they commit. I am not, and I will never claim to be an expert, but one of the things I noticed while researching profiling is that much of it can be common sense in the context of what happened. Common sense can be relative. There is no real common sense when talking about murder and the people that commit it, but you can kind of put yourself in their shoes if you really try. The problem with that is if you have never worked in that field or had experienced the sight of a real crime scene, getting into that role is difficult and, quite frankly, scary. I don't want to know what that jerk was thinking! I don't want to see those images in my head! But I guess if you truly want to figure out the type of individual that could commit the murder, you have to try.

The evening is winding down. The crowd in the alley is filing out of the building. People say their goodbyes with a yell or a wave across the parking lot, slam their doors, and hurriedly press on the gas to get to the exit. It's been a long night for a Tuesday, and it's time to go home. The morning alarm clock will be ringing in a blink of an eye. It's like a time-lapse photo, each picture frame the empty spaces in the parking lot increasing until only a few cars remain. The busy intersection of Route 4 and South Gilmore Road is like the aftermath of one of those movies about the Earth's destruction. Not much movement on the streets and the calm, cool air gives off the feeling of both the serenity of a still, moonlit night and the crisp chill of fear.

We really do not know when and where that fatal interaction took place, but we do know Laney left sometime around twelve thirty a.m. Maybe in fear of driving thirty minutes home under the influence, Laney made her last call to her boyfriend to tell him she was going to make the shorter drive to his house. Supposedly, the few patrons who were still enjoying the night didn't see her leave the bar. Somehow, after a night where many remember the "hot" girl in the bowling alley, no one saw her leave? Well, someone did.

Did they slip into action because they saw her stumble to the front door?

Did she go to the restroom one last time and evil followed?

Where in the dark did the wolf expose himself?

Unfortunately, we will never know this until he is uncovered, and maybe not even then. There were no cameras inside or outside the bowling alley in 1997. There was no way to track her movements, other than speaking to those present that night. Twenty-five —actually now twenty-six—years can distort the memories of those who noticed her that night. How did she slip out?

The bowling alley has a strange structural design in the front of the building.

The bar has a picture window in the front that shows the parking lot toward the large sign with its 1970s neon arrow pointing toward the entrance to the bowling lanes. Just outside that window to the right, if walking out, is a bump-out with entrance doors on both sides. This bump-out blocks the view of the rest of the parking lot from the bar window. Anything that happens beyond the entrance will only be seen by individuals in the parking lot or those entering and exiting the alley.

It's twelve thirty a.m., and the bowling leagues have been over for about an hour. The crowd has dwindled down to the sparse gathering in the bar. No one has passed through the doors for a while, and the chances of being seen making a move toward Laney has gone down exponentially.

If the killer is in front of the building as Laney walks out to her car, he has to be smooth in his approach. He can't just jump out of the darkness to startle her because that will draw attention. He may have had an interaction inside with Laney. She may have kindly spoken to him or possibly he's the one she harshly rejected. Either way, he has to be cool. Laney has been there a while, and the drinks have taken effect. Moving slowly to her car, she possibly has trouble getting her keys ready to put in the door. He slowly walks toward her, checking around to make sure no one else is there. Laney hasn't seen him yet, and she is unsuspecting of anyone near her. Maybe he walks up and nicely asks, "Can I help you?" Maybe he's more aggressive. Possibly, he tries to convince her he's a good dude and wants to get to know her better or he uses a ruse of needing a ride somewhere to get into her car. What he must do is not draw attention, because there are still people in the bar and possibly in the parking lot who could see him if she fights back.

Low lighting and no cameras make it the right time and place to make a move. Somehow he gets into her car in the dark void of the back of the bowling alley. He makes an excuse to get her to stop the car. Then he strikes, reaching across the car to force himself upon her. Laney fights back, pushing him away, then tries to escape the vehicle to run back toward the alley for help. He jumps out, knowing he's in trouble now. He has to stop her from screaming or running for assistance. Disoriented, she runs to get away, possibly toward the tall grass in the small field between the bowling alley and the business just up the hill. The wolf has separated his prey and now has to chase it before it gets away. He catches her, possibly holds her close or holds her down in that dark, grassy field, squeezing her tight or covering her mouth so not to break the sounds of silence. The struggle continues for a few minutes, then she stops moving.

*Oh no! What have I done?* screams loud in his head. Panic begins to set in; fight-or-flight is making him sick to his stomach. *Fuck!* What to do next? He can't go inside and tell anyone; then they will know he was doing something he shouldn't have been doing. They will know he killed her. *I gotta do something with her*, echoes through his head. He decides to hide her, but what to do with the car? The car cannot be seen in the parking lot because they would know it was him.

Here is where things are hard to predict.

What did he do with Laney's body?

Did he put her back in her car, then move the car to a nearby location to hide it?

Did he leave her hidden in those tall grasses behind the alley, then move the car?

Did he put her in the car and drive her to the river?

There are many problems with each of these situations, but he had to do something. If he left her in the grass, he took the risk of someone seeing her. It was dark, maybe the darkness of the night would conceal her, but the sun would come up. If he put her back in the car, he would have to hide it or dispose of both her and the car very quickly. But time is an issue. If he was there with friends, how would he explain his sudden departure from the alley? If he had his car in the parking lot and he left to hide her and her car, how would he get back to his? So many things had to be rushing through his mind. His heart had to be racing, like that of the narrator of Edgar Allen Poe's "The Tell-Tale Heart."

The scramble was under way. Finding a way out was a priority, but what did that entail? He had to get her and the car away from the bowling alley. Could he hide it in an adjacent parking lot? There were two apartment complexes in short walking distance from the bowling alley. Could he put her in the car so that no one could see her, then leave it in one of those nearby parking lots? If he did this, he could easily walk back to the bowling alley in a short period of time, but he then must begin his web of lies to keep his actions covered.

We know that Laney ended up in the rough waters of the Ohio River.

How did she get to the river to be found thirty-one days later?

Did the killer come back later in the morning of December 10th to retrieve her and the car, then take them both to either the Great Miami or Ohio Rivers?

If so, would they be able to complete this undertaking alone or would they need help?

To me, this seems like a daunting task. It would take a great deal of planning to get her car, with her in it, take it to the river, dispose of both, then return to where the nightmare had begun. The perp could have taken care of the first part of the feat, but he would most likely need someone to come get him to return to his vehicle. Did he draw someone else into his web? Did he tell that person what was going on or did he surround himself with more deceit? If he told, he now had to hope this person was going to be loyal and stay quiet for the rest of their lives. Who would do this? Who could keep this a secret for twenty-six years and counting? It had to be someone extremely close to him or he would be looking in his rearview mirror for the rest of his life. If his lies worked on this individual, then he would only have to keep his mouth shut until his deathbed. Either way, the voices in his head have to be lingering at all times. Each time her story is brought back to light, his heart rate has to race in fear he will be stripped of his sheep's clothing and the sins of his past will be exposed.

This scenario is under the premise Laney left through the front door. What if she didn't go out the front door? We discussed throughout the book the attention Laney drew all night from those in the bar. If she was the most beautiful thing to pass through those doors for quite some time, then I find it hard to believe no one would have noticed her going out the front door. She'd been stared at by everyone at some point during the night. There was no way she went out the front without notice. If that is the case, where did she go? From her autopsy report, we know that Laney had been drinking heavily for the few hours she was there. If she was like most people who have been drinking like that, she would have had to go to the restroom many times during the night. As a matter of fact, our witness from the "Group of Six" told us she apologized to Laney in the restroom for Wayne's behavior. The restrooms are in the bowling alley toward the side door leading to the dark side of the building. As the night progressed, the number of people in the bowling alley section of the building had continuously decreased to the point where going to the restroom could seem like a lonely endeavor. The restrooms are a pretty long walk from the bar, and they had a narrow hallway that hid them from workers at the front desk trying to close up for the evening.

The loner, who may or may not be a regular, is still hiding at the end of the bar. As he pictures himself with Laney, he begins to watch her every move. She moves toward the door of the bar that leads to that front bump-out and the front desks of the alley. Just outside the door to the left is the payphone she will use to make that last phone call.

The loner walks out behind her, watching her movements in the hope that it's nearing time to make the move. How can he get her alone? Hauntingly, standing close to her while she's on the phone, he hears her tell Mike she is about to leave. Now the urge is raging and the time to take action is getting even closer.

She walks back into the bar, possibly brushing up against him along the way. His blood rushes through his veins. He slips back to his bar stool as she goes back inside to say goodbye to Shad. She obviously is showing signs of having a bit too much to drink, and instead of going toward the front door, she goes in the direction of the door that leads to the bowling alley. This is the natural path to go to the restroom one more time before hitting the road.

The loner again slowly slithers off his bar stool to follow her out the door. As he enters the alley, he notices that no one is around. He maneuvers his way past the front desk toward the restrooms. Laney disappears into the narrow, dark hallway to the restrooms. The lights in the alley have now been dimmed because the lanes are closed for the night. He walks into that hallway, checking to see if he can see or hear anyone else in the restrooms. Silence! Now is the time. As Laney walks out of the ladies' room, our loner is waiting in the shadows of the dark hallway. He may try to make small talk or simply walk up behind her. Laney could yell or even walk very quickly toward the front desk, but why doesn't she? What if the loner has something that would make sure she cooperates? In a sudden grab of the arm and the thrust of an object into her ribs, the loner now has gotten what he wants from that night. He's close to Laney, whether she wants him to be or, more likely, not. The side door is fifteen feet away from the restrooms, and it would be easy to guide her out of the alley with little noise or effort. Laney was a fighter, but maybe not so much with something pressed against her side.

He and Laney enter into the darkness of the side parking lot. If they ran into someone, Laney may have tried to send them a signal of her danger, but they didn't catch the clue. It was after midnight, so it is conceivable that there was no one on that side of the building. He gently but forcefully pushes her to the back of the building. They are alone. He begins to make her do things he fantasized all night while in the bar, but Laney says, "HELL NO!" She hits him in a spot that will render him helpless long enough to try to get away. Again, like in the previous scenario, she's disoriented and runs to be running. The loner catches her, and now he is pissed. She can't do that to him. This was his fantasy, and damn it, he's going to fulfill it. The problem he did not foresee was that Laney is tough. She is going to fight until she cannot fight anymore. He struggles to subdue her with a military-like choke hold to keep her quiet. Then she goes limp. Thinking she has only passed out, he starts to walk away with the idea of slipping into the dark night. Then he realizes she isn't moving at all. He tries to shake her but no response. "Damn it!" He panics and begins to pace back and forth, trying to figure what to do next. He could run, but he realizes there may be some evidence on her that can be traced back to him. He sees the lump of her car keys in her back pocket and reaches in to get them. He has to get rid of her. He walks slowly toward the front of the parking lot in search of her car. He tried the keys in the few cars that were left in the parking lot. He places the key into each door until the lock turns. He jumps into her car, places it in reverse, and slowly drives to the back of the building without being noticed. He stops to put Laney's lifeless body into the car, then drives out of the back of the parking lot onto Gilmore Road.

Where did he go after leaving the parking lot?

He has a car that's not his with a dead body in it. What did he do next?

Did he drive around until he figured out his best option?

Did he park the car somewhere no one would notice until he could plot his next move?

There is another scenario that has to be considered. Laney may have either been forced into her car or coerced to let someone in, and the crime didn't happen at the bowling alley. There was a witness who came forward shortly after her disappearance to say they had seen Laney in her car driving south on Route 4. This witness went on to say they saw a large man in the car with her, wearing a black cowboy hat, and it appeared as if she was under duress. There was another witness who stated she saw a black Honda Del Sol speeding by her heading on South Gilmore Road, but as she turned into her apartment complex, she lost sight of it. Maybe Laney was taken from the bowling alley, by either a complete stranger or someone she knew, and whatever happened to her occurred far away from Fairfield. In any of these situations, the same set of circumstances had to be performed for the killer to make sure he was never caught.

1. The suspect had to figure out how to find a way to hide the car in a place it would never be found.
2. The suspect had to get Laney's body somewhere close to or in the river shortly after her death.
3. The suspect had to either perform these tasks alone or trust someone to keep a secret for the rest of their lives.
4. The suspect, if still in the area, has been able to suppress his demons for twenty-six years, telling no one of his actions.
5. The suspect may have left town under the ruse of straightening up his life shortly after leaving Laney in the cold December weather to never be found. This person may have returned several years later when news

of her disappearance started to fade into the shadows of a cold case.

Unfortunately, Laney left the bar area alone. In the shadows of the night, evil took advantage of a young woman with so much life to live. Someone decided it was more important to fulfill his fantasy than let this beautiful woman live out her dreams. I don't think this individual's plan was to kill Laney, but things got out of control really fast. Maybe he thought he was cool enough to change her mind about spending time with him, and she wanted no part of it. He lost control as his anger became rage. She unexpectedly fought back with a vengeance he had never seen before.

Maybe he tried a method he had used previously to scare unsuspecting females to commit acts they normally would not, especially with a guy like him. But Laney was different. She didn't fear him, even if he showed her a deadly weapon. He had to do something, but again, I'm not sure murder is what he had in mind.

It doesn't really matter why this monster committed this crime; the fact is he did it. The deceit has lasted for twenty-six years. He has been able to live his life under the shadows for all of this time. He may have gone on to get married, have kids, and find a career, all the milestones in life that were taken away from Laney. I have a feeling the stress of knowing what he did made it difficult at first to go on with life without worrying each day the lies would be exposed. As the years have passed, it has become easier, as the unmasking of his sins seems to be less and less likely.

The troubled life he led before could have had an effect on his actions of that night. Maybe to him the pain of knowing what he had done had scared him into straightening out his life. Fearing he would be unveiled as a murderer, he laid low, faced his demons, and kept quiet for twenty-six years. In Kennedy and Hilling's *Solving Cold Cases: Investigations Techniques and Protocol*, the writers describe how cold case investigators should look carefully at the behaviors of individuals after the crime has occurred. "Look for major shifts in behavior. Determine which suspect's life has deteriorated since the murder as well as those occasions when the suspect straightens his life out for the better" (Kennedy and Hilling, p. 31). In my research into Laney's abduction and murder, there appear to have been a couple of persons of interest that need to be evaluated under these criteria.

I know the killer thinks he has gotten away with it, but I still believe it has to be sitting deep in his memory. Maybe it doesn't surface all the time, but it has to creep back in when driving by the river or seeing a bowling alley late at night. I believe the police have spoken with this person, but he was able to slip away, hiding in plain sight.

One day, this sheep will be stripped of its soft covering to bare the rough, rabid wolf who could only be seen in the dark. Laney's story has been unfinished for far too long. Her celebration of life still hangs in the purgatory of a cold case. We will keep poking around until we find that piece of information that will allow her to rest in peace. One day, the steel trap hidden under the leaves will clamp down on the leg of the wolf, holding it until justice can be served.

# 9

# Serial?

**"It's a wicked world, and when a clever man turns his brain to crime it is the worst of all."**
— "The Adventure of the Speckled Band" (1892)

IN THE WORLD of true crime, it's human nature to be intrigued by death. It is also human nature to be enthralled with those that see death as a fantasy. Unfortunately, there have been an outrageous number of books written about the likes of Ted Bundy, John Wayne Gacy, BTK, and so many more serial killers. Many have had miniseries and documentaries chronicling their lives and horrible acts of violence. My great friend and forensic science teaching colleague, Paul Barry, and I were having this conversation not too long ago. Why is it that the killer gets all the attention, while the victims get lost in the sick fascination we all have with these vile pieces of shit? I don't know what it is, but man, it pisses me off. The bad thing about it is that it's almost impossible not to get drawn into the idea of trying to figure out what goes on in the demented brains of those who think they have the right to determine if someone lives or dies. Paul and I talked extensively about how the victims should be high-lighted, not the killer. The killer, to us, is a useless waste of flesh that will be cast into Hell to burn for eternity. Because of my research into Laney's life and tragic death, I began to reach deeper into my faith, and yeah, I do believe there is a Heaven and Hell, and these people have earned a direct flight into the fire! In the same tone, I believe the victims have been graced, without question, their angel wings. The families of the victims have to live with the departure of their loved ones every single day until they see them again in the afterlife, but while here on Earth it is a never-ending pain. Time may dull it a bit, but the sharp edge of sorrow will sneak up on them at any time. So why do we give the serial killer what he wants? Why do we grant these horrid people the attention they desire?

I don't know why we have a fascination regarding serial killers, but it is there. When you begin to look into a case involving the death of a beautiful young woman like Laney, you try hard not to fall into the pit of serial killer connections. Laney was a beautiful, petite, dark brunette whom everyone adored. She was like no other person in the world, but was she? I don't mean that in a bad way, but there are millions of young ladies that could fall into that description. Her case had to be unique, right? Well, unfortunately that is not true. Each year, women with the same wonderful charac-teristics fall to a similar fate. They came in contact with a demon who couldn't suppress the urge to take control of a gorgeous woman, then squeeze the life out of her. STOP! Don't go down that rabbit hole. Focus on what we know, and use logic to zero in on the most likely person who could have done something like the murder of Laney. Laney is not only a name on a long list of souls taken by a monster. She is special. She cannot be lumped into that category of a serial killer's infamy. What came next, as farfetched as it seemed, had to be looked into.

Was Laney the victim of the worst type of human being alive?

Did Laney come in contact with, I hate to say it, a serial killer?

In our initial search, we found the story of Melissa Witt. It is on a website called "Who Killed Missy Witt?" The website is run by LaDonna Humphrey, an investigative journalist and private investigator out of Arkansas. On the site, she told the story of the disappearance and murder of a beautiful young woman. LaDonna would later go on to write a tremendous book, *The Girl I Never Knew*, and film a documentary highlighting her work to find Melissa's killer. As I stated earlier in this book, this site actually drew me to Laney's case. LaDonna goes on to tell about Melissa in such great detail, but what caught my eye was the picture of Laney at the bottom of the page. It was the same picture that has covered most newspapers, TV broadcasts, and billboards in the Cincinnati area. The cowboy hat, blue-and-white striped cropped sweater, and the blue jeans. The image of a western cowgirl, dropped into Ohio. You couldn't help but look, but then the story lured me even more. Melissa, like Laney, had been taken from a bowling alley parking lot. Their bodies were found fifty to sixty miles away from where they were last known to be. Their facial features were mysteriously similar, and their smile was hard to look away from. The bowling alleys were similar in location, with busy roads and car dealerships on all sides. A short drive would put the killer on a highway to make a quick escape from the alley.

Could Laney and Missy's cases actually be connected?

During the 1970s, '80s, and '90s, highway serial killers were frighteningly common. There was the I-71 killer labeled Dr. No. He traveled up and down I-71, which passes really close to Fairfield. Could Laney have run into this monster? Chances are slim considering Dr. No picked up prostitutes at truck stops, then disposed of them along I-71 as if they were trash. Laney wasn't a prostitute, and I would venture to guess she had never been to a truck stop. Most the highway serials were truckers or individuals that had to traverse the web of interstates for work. They were monsters of opportunity, taking advantage of individuals that had no other means to travel. There was the I-5 murderer, the I-40 murderer, the redhead murderer, and so many more, but there we go again, talking about the killers and not the victims. It's so hard to not roll down that hill right into the mud puddle of sick shit serial killers do. It is almost impossible not to try to hang a murder like Laney's on a serial killer. It is easy to make up connections to other murders because there will always be some similarities to others cases. With all the documentaries, social media outlets, and articles written about these sick people, we have been kind of trained to think that the murder of a young, beautiful woman has to be the work of a serial. We tried not to get caught up in this wild goose chase, but we had to look into those connections LaDonna made between Missy and Laney.

We knew we had to reach out to LaDonna. I sent Evan on the hunt for contact information, and like always, he had an email within minutes. We drafted an email on November 8, 2018, and with a click, it was sent. Then we waited, and waited, and waited. I did not realize until later how busy LaDonna was working on her books and the documentary, *Uneven Ground*, about Melissa, but then on November 24, 2018, the relationship with Mrs. Humphrey would start the wheels rolling for many things to come over the next six years, eventually leading to the writing of this book. We needed to know why Laney was placed on the same website with Melissa. It seemed a bit farfetched to us at first. Laney was in Fairfield, Ohio, and Melissa was in Fort Smith, Arkansas. The distance between the two cities on a good day would take nearly eleven hours by car. That seemed a long way for these cases to be connected.

Eventually, we would get the opportunity to speak with LaDonna. She laid out the details of each case as we listened intently. Melissa was a young, beautiful brunette, the same as Laney. Both women were abducted from a parking lot, more specifically a bowling alley parking lot. Melissa went missing on December 1, 1994, while Laney went missing on December 10, 1997. Melissa's body was found on January 13, 1995, sixty miles away from where she went missing , and Laney was found on January 11, 1998, nearly sixty miles from her place of abduction site. Melissa put up a fight to escape from her abductor, and Laney would never go down without a battle.

Could these cases really be related?

Was there a serial killer traveling across the country with a trigger that motivated him to kill in the month of December?

As we continued to talk about the cases, LaDonna hit us with a bombshell, which is in her book, about a man named Larry Swearingen. At the time of our discussion, Larry was on death row in Texas for the murder of Melissa Trotter. Melissa Trotter went missing on December 8, 1998, and her body was found on January 2, 1999. She had similar characteristics to both Laney and Melissa Witt. Her body was found in the Sam Houston National Forest, which according to Google Earth is about thirty to forty miles away from where she was last seen. All three victims were most likely strangled from behind. Were these strange coincidences, or was there something there? At first glance, it didn't seem possible that someone could move from Arkansas to Ohio, then to Texas, to abduct these women, strangle them, and leave them out in the wilderness.

As we continued to look down the serial killer microscope, we realized maybe it was possible. When you look at the maps of our country, the highways appear like those yarn strings of an old detective movie, each connecting a clue to the suspect and victim in the plot. There are so many ways a person can make their way from one coast to the other in a matter of days. If Larry is one of our possible links to this puzzle, he had several years to make the rounds. It makes you wonder if there are more victims out there that met their end in the month of December. Were some bodies found in January, but the yarn was never connected? Were some bodies never found?

We are not accusing Larry of Laney's or Melissa Witt's murders, because we have no proof he committed these atrocious acts. We haven't been able to connect him to the Fairfield, Ohio, area, but we also do not have proof he wasn't. It is compelling to look at the possibility of Larry as a serial killer, but it is easy to use a serial killer as the scapegoat of crimes like this, because it would make more sense to us, rather than think it could have been someone close to each victim. Larry also didn't help himself. He was a convicted felon, and many of his acts of violence were toward women. Larry Swearingen was executed for the death of Melissa Trotter in 2019. He claimed his innocence all the way up until they inserted the needle into his arm.

We focused on those similarities with these three cases for quite a while, but we then also had to look at the differences. Both Melissa Trotter and Missy Witt were sexually assaulted, but it was not completely confirmed if Laney was. Do I think sexual assault was the goal of the killer? Yes, I do, but why was it not completed? Melissa Trotter and Missy Witt were both found in the middle of a national forest, while Laney was floating in the Ohio River. Missy Witt was found naked, while Laney and Melissa Trotter were both found with clothes on. At this time, it cannot be determined if these cases are linked. Could they be? Maybe. Is it likely? I don't think so, but who knows? Until we can find concrete evidence, we will have to keep looking at all the options, leaving Larry Swearingen as a possibility.

Evan and I put Larry aside for the time being, but while digging more, we came across a web sleuth's website that had the pictures of young females who could have been victims of a convicted murderer by the name of Chris Below. Unfortunately, when we first started this process, we definitely had no idea what we were doing. Since finding that page on the internet, it has changed, and finding the exact link has become difficult. The premise of the link was the pictures and brief stories of young women who had gone missing in the Ohio, Indiana, and Kentucky area in the mid- to late 1990s. Names like Heather Teague, twenty-three, August 26, 1995—Spottsville, Kentucky; Shaylene Farrell, eighteen, August 8, 1994—Piqua, Ohio; Kristina Porco, sixteen, November 29, 1986—Hilton Head Island, South Carolina; Kathern Fetzer, twenty-six, November 26, 1991—Medina, Ohio; and Alana "Laney" Gwinner, twenty-three, December 10, 1997—Fairfield, Ohio were listed on that page, and many had not been found. Chris was known to travel for his job and was found to have traveled in the area that many of these women had been taken. Were we looking at another serial killer situation?

Could Chris have taken Laney that night and dropped her off by the river?

We had to look into it. As we researched Chris Below, we came across an article about the kidnapping of Heather Teague. She was taken from a Kentucky state park parking lot, never to be seen again. In her case, there was a man who lived across the lake that happen to be filming the lake that morning and caught the abduction on film. The only problem was he was too far away to get a good picture of the suspects or their vehicles. It appeared there were two abductors and one had a distinct gait. The authorities were closing in on these monsters, and one was Chris. Unfortunately, the witness could not completely confirm it was him, and video analysis of his gait was not enough to connect him to the crime. Detectives were ready to question a close friend of Chris' when he saw the police on his tail. This friend proceeded to speed down the road to his driveway, where he pulled a gun and shot himself in the head. The only person that could put Chris in that park the day Heather went missing was now gone.

Chris was a prime suspect in many of these missing women, but one in particular would be his demise. Kathern Fetzer was rumored to be having an affair with Chris. They worked together, and the affair had gone on for quite some time before Kathern decided it needed to stop. Unfortunately, for Kathern that was a deadly decision. As we continued looking at Chris, we came across the name of an officer that refused to let him get away with murder. Officer Scott Thomas was like a bloodhound on the scent. He knew Chris was responsible for the disappearance of Kathern, and he wasn't going to stop until he got him to say it. Detective Thomas hounded all of Chris' relatives and followed his every move. He drove thousands of miles, talking to anyone that knew Below. The pressure was mounting.

We knew we had to speak with Detective Thomas. He was a direct link to someone that may have been responsible for Laney's death. Chris Below, although only convicted of Kathern's murder, may have been a serial killer, and Laney could have been one of his victims. The search began to find Detective Thomas. We searched Google. We searched Facebook. We searched county records of Medina, Ohio. We called the police department in that area, but Detective Thomas had retired many years prior to our inquiry.

Where was this guy?

Would he talk to us?

Did he know if Chris could have killed Laney or any of those other girls on that list?

We seemed to be hitting roadblock after roadblock. Then on November 29, 2018, I decided to look at LinkedIn to see if I could find Scott Thomas, the former police detective. At first, a few different people came up with the same Scott Thomas name. Which one was the right one? Then I found one that was listed as Scott Thomas, Retired Director of Public Safety/Public Works. Could this be him? I wrote a quick note to let him know what Evan and I were doing and requested an invite to his LinkedIn page. Two hours later, we got an acceptance from Scott, and he responded to our question:

Hi Randy, we certainly can talk about Christopher Below. You can give me a call.

YES! We found him! Now we could get down to business. We wanted to know everything we could about Scott.

How long was he a detective?

How did he catch Chris?

Did he have any information about the possibility of Chris being involved in Laney's case?

We were talking with a real detective who put a possible serial killer behind bars. We were hearing the story straight from the man who put Chris away for many years. Scott has a very distinctive voice, stern but kind at the same time. You could tell he was proud of his work as a detective. He also loves to teach others the investigative process, because, in his words, "we don't teach that enough to kids in high school." He commended us for our efforts and offered his assistance without hesitation. Scott truly wanted to help us work through this case because he feels the more eyes looking at a case, the better the chance of solving it, even if it's not the eyes of law enforcement.

Detective Thomas took us through the many years he worked on Kathern Fetzer's case and how he had to track Chris Below down until he was put behind bars for her murder. The story was captivating, and he kept us on the edge of our seats about the many miles he traveled, the states he traversed, and the moment he got Below to admit he had murdered Kathern.

When Detective Thomas felt the time was right, he moved in to question Chris. Trying to be the tough guy, Chris tried to keep his mouth shut until his current girlfriend, who knew the bad side of him, was asked by Detective Thomas to go into the room with Chris and play the sympathy card of Kathern's family. She quietly walked into the interrogation room with tears in her eyes and began to engage Chris in a heartfelt conversation about what he had done with Kathern. She empathized with him about how he felt when she cut him off from the relationship. He began to squirm a bit in his chair. She talked about how it must be hard to have that looming over his head. Becoming agitated, he slumped back in his chair but still refused to admit anything. Then she quietly said to him, "What about her family? How do you think her parents feel?" In a sudden burst, Chris blurted out, "I DON'T GIVE A FUCK ABOUT HER FAMILY!" At that point, Chris knew he made a mistake, and so did Detective Thomas. Armed with that recorded statement, Detective Thomas got him to admit he killed Kathern Fetzer. The question still remained: Did he kill those other girls, including Laney?

Scott discussed some of the other cases Chris may have been involved with and recalled speaking with Butler County Sheriff's Detective Frank Smith about the possibility of Below being in Fairfield in 1997. Through their thorough investigation, it appeared as if Chris was most likely not in the Fairfield area during the time of Laney's disappearance. The circumstances of Laney's case did not fit the profile of most of the alleged cases Chris may have been linked to. Later, our research confirmed the conversation Detective Thomas had with Detective Smith. It was also confirmed that Chris Below was questioned for Laney's case, but it came to light he had no knowledge of the Fairfield area or of Laney.

Dead end! Or was it?

Even though the Chris Below lead didn't lead us to her killer, and Larry Swearingen could not be completely confirmed, it did lead us to resources that would prove to be invaluable. Talking with Scott Thomas and LaDonna Humphrey was an experience Evan and I had never thought we would ever have. His knowledge and insight into the investigative process and her tenacity to find the truth taught us so many lessons on what to do and what not to do in our quest to find Laney's killer. Both allowed us to bounce ideas off them. The two of them would give us ideas of where to look next. Scott would have been a terrific teacher because he never told us exactly what to do; he would question the purpose of our next move. LaDonna would give us tips on how to dig for answers in a sea of so many unknowns. Both would play devil's advocate in some situations, to make sure we were looking at the case from all perspectives. We were experiencing the ultimate education by doing it in real-time with professionals guiding us along the way.

Something was happening.

It was as if Laney was whispering in our ear, "Don't stop! There is so much more to do."

## 10

## Atypical Opportunities

**"Embrace the uncertainty; it's where miracles happen"**
— Unknown

WHEN EVAN and I started on this journey, we had no idea where it would lead. We started talking with people we probably would have never spoken to without this endeavor of finding Laney's killer. It began as a challenge to find information. As we continued speaking with her friends and family, and authorities, it evolved into so much more. The real emotions expressed by those close to Laney as we asked difficult questions began to hit hard. My Joe Friday, "Just the facts, ma'am," attitude quickly melted away, and the anvil of heartache was now crushing my chest. Laney was not merely that girl in the picture anymore. She was a real person with family, friends, goals, and dreams. She reminded me of my own daughters, and the pain of losing them to the hands of a killer was unimaginable. I figuratively stepped into the shoes of her parents. I started to imagine the paralyzing fear of not knowing where she was as the days and weeks passed. My eyes began to well with tears as I pictured the police officers walking to the front door to deliver the devastating news that her body was found in the cold, muddy waters of the Ohio River. I felt the weakness in my knees that I'm sure overtook Laney's mother as she collapsed to the ground in despair. It wasn't just a story of a missing and murdered young lady. It was Laney's story, and I couldn't let it go.

Many nights, Evan and I would spend three, four, five hours after school searching for people to talk to about Laney. Activities like running off copies of maps, looking into weather data, reading articles, and marking water locations to search took up an enormous amount of our lives after we realized Laney was more than what happened to her. We became immersed in the details, often not realizing the sun had set hours prior. Like the ivy on the walls at Wrigley Field, names, phone numbers, Facebook profiles, and any information we could find covered the many whiteboards that surrounded my classroom. The real work began when we spoke to Laney's friend Joy. We had to prepare questions that would give us pertinent information to allow us to establish victimology. The questions had to be direct but also empathetic. Joy was opening up to us about something so tragic, and we had to build rapport with her if we wanted answers. This was intimidating, to say the least. I have spoken with people who have lost loved ones to accidents, disease, or age. Hell, I have lost two of my sisters well before their time. But this was different.

How do you talk to people about a murdered loved one?

We researched so much information about the case before making that initial call. We created timelines. We labeled folders with names of important people related to the case, like Sergeant Ed Roberts, Detective Frank Smith, Joy, Karrie, Angie, and Brittany. We looked into the names of individuals mentioned in articles, websites, and Facebook pages. We critically read comments on all those media outlets, trying to find things that could be of interest.

Why would that person say this in a comment?

How did this person know her?

Was there something diabolical about that comment?

We studied books about gathering information in a criminal case. We went to our resource officer in our building to get advice on where to go and who to talk to. At times the work became overwhelming. The information was abundant yet scarce at the same time. We knew when we started to speak with those connected to Laney or the case we better be prepared. This wasn't a research project; this was a human project. In other words, we were serious, and the goal was to at least bring Laney's story back into the spotlight, even for a short moment in time. Laney, like all of the victims of cold cases, deserved to be highlighted in a way that could render some answers to some very tough questions. Time doesn't stand still and, like thousands of other cases, hers was slipping into the darkness, as those involved were losing details into the depths of their memories, and, unfortunately, some had succumbed to the inevitable passing of life.

Joy spoke openly with us, showing her emotions and the pain she feels to this day. She, like all of Laney's friends at the time, had a bit of survivor's remorse. How could someone so close have been taken from them this way? Sometimes feeling guilty about not being able to go out with Laney that night really hit hard for Joy—and others. The what-ifs of, "If only I was there that night." Most people who lose someone, especially if circumstances could have been different, go through this, but this was the first time, at least for me and I'm sure for Evan, that we witnessed the guilt felt by those who really had no control over the events of that night. It was eye opening, to say the least.

Joy gave us the names of other friends, including Angie and Karrie. Inseparable friends at the time Laney died, those two would open our eyes to the pain and heartache that will not go away. From the changing of birthday celebrations because it was the same day as her disappearance to the annual posts in loving memory of Laney on social media, the agony was evident. But we had to talk with them. We had to know everything we could about Laney before that awful night. We needed to know where she would go, who she would hang out with, what type of person she was in confrontations, how her family life and her financial situation were. All this information was needed to develop the many possibilities of how that night turned so catastrophic.

Each conversation was more interesting than the previous one. The information was critical to our next steps, who to talk with and who not to talk with. What direction of questioning should be taken with the next person? Each conversation telling us more, keeping us busy searching for that minute, well-hidden answer to what may have happened that night. Each person having their own speculation of who possibly could have done something so awful. Some believed it could be someone she knew, while others thought it was simply the wrong place to be with an opportunistic monster.

Angie introduced us to Brittany, who only became friends with Angie's group after Laney's death. She, like the others, could not let it go and would do whatever it took to bring Laney's killer to justice. In my soul, I believe that Laney always wanted her rodeo friends to meet Brittany, and through the darkness of her death, she shined a light from Heaven to make sure they would all meet someday. They are now eternally connected to each other through Laney's angelic embrace.

Brittany was able to tell us about a period in Laney's life that wasn't so pleasant. Laney's smile caught Brittany's attention when they lived in the same apartment complex, but it was Laney's internal and external scars that drew them close. Brittany watched as Laney struggled through that rough, abusive relationship with Matthew.

Through her friends, we began to see the ups and downs of Laney's life. The beautifully painted portrait of her as compared to who she really was. As we gathered more information and talked to more people, the true portrait of Laney started to emerge from the bright colors of the great things happening in her life to the black-and-gray shadows that hid the heartaches life can bring.

Armed with an overwhelming amount of background information about Laney, from her kind heart to her love interests, both good and bad, to her professional growth, we knew we had to know more about other parts of her story. Through an emotional conversation with David, Laney's brother, I was able to get a copy of the autopsy report. It was an education in itself. There were terms I had to look up to understand. The sheer level of detail in the document was like reading a novel for a science nerd like me. Even after looking into the medical terminology, we still needed clarity in what we were actually reading. We spoke with Carol Lehman, our Anatomy and Physiology teacher at Mason High School, to get an idea of the true meaning of the report. She was tremendously helpful, but we felt we needed a specialist to confirm what we thought we knew. We decided to call the local coroner in our county.

The county coroner was great and fielded our questions without delay. Through the lens of science, we now had an idea of the trauma Laney experienced right before her death. This gave us an idea of the mindset of the killer. The snapshot of the type of person who could have fallen into a state of frustration or anger to the point of murder was developing.

Unfortunately, our local coroner was going strictly off the information we were giving them about the copy of Laney's autopsy we had in our possession. They did not have the pictures, the step-by-step procedures, or the actual experience of performing her autopsy, so much of the information they gave us was based on their experience with similar cases they had performed. We really needed to contact someone who had been there or who had at least studied the photos from her autopsy.

Then we realized, why don't we go to the proverbial "horse's mouth" to get the real answers we were seeking? Dr. Charles Stephens, MD, the medical examiner of northern Kentucky's St. Luke Hospital, was listed as the person who performed Laney's autopsy. Evan started digging, like a dog for a bone, to find anything we could find about Dr. Stephens. Bingo! We found him. The age, location, and professional background of the Dr. Stephens we found was perfect. That had to be him. We found a phone number, and I was beginning to type it in my phone, when Evan said, "Wait!" He had found an obituary of Dr. Stephens, long time ME of northern Kentucky. We had just missed our opportunity, as the fine doctor had passed only two days prior to us finding him. This was a reality check for us in the realm of investigating a cold case. We now understood one issue that cold case detectives face today, TIME. As time passes, so do individuals, memories, and details. We'd hit one of our first roadblocks.

It was an opportunity to learn something new by changing directions to find others willing to speak. The key word in that last sentence was opportunity. As we spent the first few months looking for information, I suddenly realized we were engaging in a true education through real-life events. We had spoken with people that we would have never spoken to through the everyday classroom activities we were doing in my Forensic Science classes.

I had been teaching for twenty-nine years, and I had invited professionals in some of these fields to come talk to my classes about their jobs. All we asked of them were routine questions from what type of education was needed to everyday life in their job, and of course addressing the student who wanted to know the grossest thing they had ever seen. That information was important, but did we really get anything meaningful from that experience that would help us or others in the future? Probably not. Laney was giving us an experience like no other. We weren't just talking to a coroner; we were talking with them. We weren't just hearing how upset her friends and family were; we were feeling it ourselves. The pain, the intrigue, and the frustration were embedding themselves like a worm in our brains. Our mission was evolving, and we were not giving up without a fight.

Shortly after our initial conversation with Detective Thomas, retired Detective Mark Reiber sent an email to touch base about seeing our interview with Jessica Schmidt of FOX19. That email never made it to me. A year went by before Mark got my number at school and contacted me for what he thought was the second time. In reality, he wrote the email but forgot to hit send. Again, did Laney have a hand in him finally getting a hold of me? Why would someone who hadn't received a reply a year ago try again? Thankfully, he did. Mark's connection to the case was strange, if not a bit creepy. He had moved into the Gwinner house, the very house Laney had grown up in. Was it eerie or was it divine? I'm not sure, but it definitely caught our attention as we began speaking with him. Mark was highly interested and began to get into the case just as much as we were. He also had that strange feeling as if Laney was reaching out to him to join us. Mark described a dream he had in which we found her car in a local pond, and it was in great condition for a car submerged for twenty-plus years. He remembered saying in the dream, "It was so obvious, how did we miss it?"

Was Laney bringing us all together for a reason?

Why was Mark so persistent in reaching out to us?

Retired detectives are like athletes; when their career is over, it is hard to walk away. They are adrenaline junkies who live for the hunt of the bad guy. At times, Mark would ask me questions as if I was a suspect, searching for all that I knew about Laney and her case. He was looking for things we may have found that could help him guide us in the right direction. These kinds of questions led us to think differently, to consider all the possibilities. It was a great learning experience for Evan and me.

As civilians, we mostly see detective work through a television lens. The bad guy always makes a mistake and the dapper, well-dressed detective breaks down the door to handcuff him while reciting a witty, sarcastic statement in his ear about getting caught. This unfortunately is not real-world detective work. Real detective work is long, agonizing hours away from their families chasing down leads. It is sifting through all the bullshit that surrounds the case. It's cutting through all the red tape to try to bring someone to justice for a crime. And what really sucks is that sometimes it leaves the detectives in the dark, no different than when they started the investigation. Evan and I were getting the experience of a lifetime by talking Laney's case through the eyes of people who had walked through the trenches of real detective work. Their attention to detail was like watching a painter turn a blank canvas into a masterpiece.

Evan and I continued to reach deep into those articles to find names of individuals we needed to speak with. Names like Detective Frank Smith from the Butler County Sheriff's Office who took over the case in 2005. We emailed Detective Smith, who at the time was running a polygraph company that was used by many police departments and federal agencies in the area. We really didn't think he would respond to us, but to our surprise, he emailed us back very quickly and actually called my phone to leave a message that he would be willing to speak with us about Laney's case. We were caught a little off guard. I sent that email thinking it would be a miracle if he responded, and we didn't get our hopes up too high. Now we had to prepare. I sat down and started writing all the questions we wanted to ask Frank, knowing he probably wouldn't answer most of them. But I learned a long time ago the worst answer he could give us was no, so go ahead and ask the question. Armed with our numbered list of questions, we confidently set up an appointment with Detective Smith at his office in downtown Hamilton, Ohio.

Hamilton was actually called Fort Hamilton in the late 1700s. It was a fort settled on the Great Miami River, used to defend against the Indians (Native Americans) as the colonies moved west. I guess you could say it was part of the Westward Expansion of the United States. The fort was named after one of the Founding Fathers of the United States of America, Alexander Hamilton. Fort Hamilton was a major route for supplies along the Great Miami and the Miami-Erie Canal. Hamilton, Ohio, has always been proud of its heritage and to this day has a monument next to the river to honor those who held that fort for so many years and to those who fought in each of the wars that followed after the formation of the United States. Like many towns of that era, it went through many changes. It went from a fort to an agricultural mecca, where farming was the life and innovative equipment was made to increase yield. The Industrial Revolution set in, and Hamilton became a place of paper factories, bank safe manufacturing, and department stores such as Elder Beerman and Sears. The town was booming, but time took its toll, and the town lost much of its manufacturing, and wealth seemed to be slipping away. Hamilton had its great days and its bad days, but today it is starting to make a comeback with the reconstruction of the downtown area.

Evan and I met after school one day to drive over to Hamilton to meet Detective Smith. The town still had all the remnants of the past, with the Soldier Monument along the river and the eerie 1700s courthouse that was under renovations to become business space and housing for the new look Hamilton was creating. The mixture of the old with the new beautiful municipal building gave you the feeling of being in a movie like *Back to the Future*. All we needed was a Delorian and a clock tower.

We parked across the street from the old Sears store, which my mother dragged me through hundreds of times. We walked to the address that Detective Smith sent us. It was an old building, with really tall ceilings, old mahogany baseboards, and an elevator that barely fit the two of us. We exited the elevator to a floor that only had one door in the hallway. It was locked, so we knocked and waited for an answer. Shortly, a buzz to let us in occurred, and we quickly pushed the door to make sure the person on the other side didn't have to hit the buzzer again. Nervously, we entered the room. A balding man, who looked as if he was full of experience and knowledge, made his way through another door. He greeted us with a firm handshake and almost a smile. He walked us into a room with two posters on opposite walls. One was a poster of all the cold cases he had closed, and the other showed the ones that still haunted him. The cases he wasn't able to solve before he retired from the sheriff's office. He told us stories about both posters, then focused on Laney, since of course we were there to talk about her.

You could tell he was heartbroken about her case. He always felt it could be solved, and I believe he still feels that way today. He then took us into the next room with an old desk you would find in the public libraries that had not been renovated since, well, the establishment of Fort Hamilton. He smiled at us and in his deep raspy voice said, "You need to turn off your cell phones and leave them in this room. No electronic devices can be taken into my office or the polygraph room, including car keys with a key fob on them." He said that with a pretty stern voice, so Evan and I quickly turned off our phones and placed them and our keys on the desk. Then he led us into the next room, his office, which was right next to the room where he performed his polygraph tests. His office was filled with files and books all over the place. Some were neatly stacked, while others looked like he had been rummaging through them right before we arrived. Then, in a true detective manner, he asked, "Do one of you have a garage door opener or car keys in your pocket?" Nervously, we checked our pockets. Neither of us had anything. He said with that detective's voice, "You better check, and I hope you don't have a recording device on you." A bit scared, we scrambled to check our pockets, but nothing.

I said, "Why do you ask that?" He stated that his electronic device monitoring system was picking up on a device in the room, and it had to be on one of us. Then it dawned on me.

"I do have an insulin pump."

He asked, "Does it have Bluetooth?"

I replied, "Yes, is that a problem?"

He then laughed a bit, as if he knew I was getting nervous, and stated, "No, but I knew you had something on you."

Then I thought to myself, *How could a building this freaking old have technology in it that could detect my pump?* It kind of freaked me out. After the interrogation about the device I had on me, we were then able to ask our questions. He was a very direct and careful man. He would tell us if we were on the right track with our questions but wouldn't hesitate to state, "No comment," if he thought we were getting too close to specific details. He was like a true crime narrator, giving us enough information to keep us searching, but not enough to spoil the ending.

Frank sat behind his desk, dispensing wisdom with that authoritative voice from his extensive career in law enforcement. He told us stories of the long hours without sleep investigating the many horrors he had seen in his career. It was like listening to your father tell war stories; every detail kept you on edge. Then, as he looked at that poster with those cold cases still unsolved, you could see the emotion in his eyes. It hurt him to know that someone was still out there who had committed those crimes. He used those posters, both the solved and unsolved, to remind him that his career as a detective and his current work with polygraphy was to help people like those on the posters.

Before we left, he offered to show us the room and chair where he performed his polygraph tests. It was an old, closet-like room. Your mood changed immediately with the dull paint color and the barred window in the corner that had plywood covering it. It felt like being in the attic of the house in the *Amityville Horror* movie. You were just waiting for the whispering voice to say, "Get out."

We asked why the window had bars and was boarded up.

He chuckled. "Well, the last guy to sit in that chair must have been lying because he tried to break the glass and pull the bars off so he could jump out." We laughed a little bit, then he told me to sit in the chair. Nervously, I did. He then, in a serious voice, said, "I have a few questions to ask you."

"Wait, what?"

Laughing, he said, "Just kidding!"

After my stomach returned to normal, I took a deep breath and sat in the chair. It was hard, cold, and very intimidating. I could see how someone who had to sit there answering questions about a murder could get messed up and make a nervous mistake, but I guess that was why there were people trained to decipher between nervousness and lying.

Our conversation was winding down. We came up with a few more questions to ask, then we thanked him for taking the time to speak with us. Detective Smith was gracious and told us good luck with our research. He offered to answer any other questions we had if he could and walked us to the door. The offer to answer any questions was probably not the best thing to say to us, because for the next five years I peppered his email with questions, ideas, and updates. He replied to some, ignored many, and delayed others until he couldn't take it anymore. He was very gracious until I probably pushed a little too far for his liking. When he ignored several of my requests in a row, I had my connections reach out to him, thinking the law enforcement links would show him that Evan and I were serious about finding Laney's killer. It backfired a bit. Detective Smith ultimately told me he would not speak to me about Laney's case again. You could tell in his voice he was irritated with me. He calmly told us to keep working on it, but he could no longer speak to us because he was afraid we would mess up the investigation. He didn't like that we had acquired the information we had, and in his stern, warm voice he ended the voicemail with, "Good luck and God Bless."

Well, crap! What could we do now?

Jessica Schmidt, our FOX19 reporter connection, told us about making a Freedom of Information Act (FOIA) request. A FOIA request is a formal written request from a citizen to a public entity, like government offices, school systems, and police departments, asking for specific information. When we wrote the FOIA, we actually thought we would be denied, considering it is still an open case. Laws in most states allow for exceptions to giving information to the public due to many reasons. In Ohio, article 149.43 states that government agencies such as police departments can deny request for a FOIA, especially if a case is still considered to be open and under investigation.

We were surprised when someone from the local authorities' office called me back and stated that he would be willing to talk to me about Laney's case. I'll call him George. George stated that Laney's case has been sitting in boxes in the storage room for nearly twenty years with not much action being taken on them. He said that it is going to take a person to admit they are the killer or someone to come forward with some information. George said he figured it wouldn't hurt to allow more eyes to look at the files to see if anything was overlooked.

I spent hours in his office, scouring through the mounds of boxes for information and listening to recordings of individuals who have been spoken to about the case. I cannot discuss the things that I heard on those tapes, but I will say that the education I was getting was tremendous. As I translated my visits to Evan, we learned why some people were interviewed and why others were not. We learned how some police officers went about asking questions to try to get crucial information about Laney's case. We were being sucked into that vortex of what happened, why it happened, and who in the hell may have done this to Laney. At times, it felt like an exercise in futility, sifting through piles of papers, some seeming to have no relevance at all. It was both intriguing and frustrating all at the same time, but Evan and I never learned as much as we have during this journey. This wasn't a curriculum lesson; this was a life lesson. This was a practice of perseverance and determination. Laney's case became a test of our will, and our will was strong.

Evan, being young, was afraid of nothing, like I used to be. But I was a bit more cautious about our steps, making sure not to overstep our bounds or get in the way of the investigation. Then I realized something through Evan's vigor: things will not change if you don't take chances along the way. The case hadn't been looked into for nearly twenty-plus years at the time we started. Maybe we were chosen to do this. Maybe Laney was guiding us to be bold, aggressive, and inquisitive to teach us that the mysteries of our world will not be found without these traits. Answers will not come if you don't seek them. As Dylan Thomas said, "Do not go gentle into that good night." We weren't going to stop and let Laney's case keep falling deeper into the darkness of that cold case file.

We found the Covington fire chief who was in the helicopter when her body was found. He is getting older now, but he remembered with great detail what he saw that day. He adamantly stated he knew it was a female body with a specific sweater on that could be seen from the air. Through his experience, he did not feel she had been in the water very long, especially since the water was flowing with such power that day.

Next, we found someone who worked for the Boone County Water Rescue Team. He wasn't very keen about giving us too much information because the case was still open but explained to us the actions of the river and what it was like on that day in 1998.

Later, through Mark's connections, we were able to speak with Sergent Purcell about his interactions with the Butler County Sheriff Investigator Frank Smith and what he felt about the pictures he had seen of Laney right after her recovery from the river. He corroborated the fire chief's sentiments, stating Laney's body did not appear to have the normal characteristics of a body in the river for thirty-one days. In our discussion, he gave me a lesson on what the body will go through in a watery grave. As described in the "May Pop" chapter, it didn't add up for her to be floating on the top of the river in January if she had been trapped in her car for all that time.

Then Chad Jones came to speak to my class about being a detective and a coroner's investigator. During breaks between classes, he noticed a notebook I had titled "Laney Gwinner." In his detective's manner, he asked me all the things I could tell him about Laney's case. Within minutes, he looked at me and said, "I think this can be solved!" Like Mark, he saw some things in the case that led him to believe that the answer was close and we had to keep shaking the tree until it fell out.

He looked at a few grainy black-and-white photos of Laney from the few autopsy photos we received in the FOIA request. He and Mark both noticed things I would never have looked for, such as marks on her neck, straw in her hair, and possible swelling that could have been premortem. I understand that detectives have to go through serious training before moving into the high-stress job of criminal investigation, but I also believe some are naturally gifted in their ability to find the details. I believed I was working with guys who had that "it" factor when it came to investigations. Every time I spoke with them, I learned something new.

Today I view Scott, Mark, and Chad as friends. Friends I would have never gotten to meet if it wasn't for Laney's connection. I continue to speak with Joy, Karrie, Brittany, and Angie about Laney and where we need to go next. We share motivating greetings, wish each other happy birthday, and congratulate each other on big life events. Laney's brother David and I share texts about our interest in old Pontiac Firebirds and Chevy Camaros. We like each other's social media posts of the great things our children are doing in their lives.

Evan and I have talked with lawyers, detectives, water rescue specialists, coroners, media personnel, and so many other individuals we never would have even thought about talking to if it wasn't for Laney. We have crawled in a river to mark a car. We have kayaked on ponds, streams, and rivers looking for any sign of her car. I personally have done a few semi-dangerous things my wife wasn't too happy about to see if we could find that one clue that will lead us or the authorities in a new direction.

Each night I go to bed with Laney's case on my mind. I revisit the information gathered by speaking with all of these new acquaintances I have made over the years. I see Laney's face from the "Justice For Laney" Facebook page and missing posters I have stared at for so long, trying to figure out what she is trying to say to me. That deep feeling in my gut is always there, and I feel it isn't only about Laney.

Why did we pick Laney's case?

We could have picked from thousands of others from the greater Cincinnati area, but we didn't.

Why?

Then one day in school, it hit me. There was so much more to do. Laney was speaking to me because she was with those thousands whose voices haven't been heard. Laney was telling us there was more work to be done!

She was telling me we needed to start a program designed to bring to light those stories that have fallen into the darkness of dusty file cabinets. Her friends and family say that they know Laney would be honored to be responsible for the education of our youth in such a real-world experience.

Through tragedy shines grace, and Laney was shining brightly.

Through Laney's grace, a movement was started, the creation of a program to educate students while bringing awareness to cold cases.

It was now time for us to begin. We decided our motto for our Cold Case MHS (Mason High School) program is "speaking for those who cannot."

# 11

# Laney's Touch

**"True education consists in the cultivation of the heart."**
— Sai Baba

EVAN and I had been working on Laney's case for probably five months when Jessica Schmidt from our local FOX19 News station called me out of the blue. She left a message on my voicemail stating she had heard about the work Evan and I had been doing and thought it would be a great story to tell. Jessica is an avid true crime buff. As stated earlier in the book, she does a segment on the news called the Crime Vault and now currently has a podcast called *Crime Vault: Beyond the Broadcast*. Like most people who are invested in true crime, she tries to bring light to stories in the greater Cincinnati area that have fallen into the dark black hole of cold cases. Jessica is a go-getter and truly digs deep into the stories she talks about on air.

She was working on a Crime Vault story about Laney after

finding some old news clips her station ran back in 1997. Unlike me, Jessica is way too young to know anything about Laney's story firsthand, so she began to dig for information like Evan and I were, and she came across Joy, a friend of Laney's. I had mentioned earlier in the book that Joy was one of the first people we reached out to because we saw her name in several articles and on a podcast. Joy passed the information about the work we were doing to Jessica, and that is how our relationship started.

Jessica is a strong advocate for us, often reaching out to people to help us. Jessica brought a cameraman and her notes to my school one night when Evan and I were working late, as we had been doing for several months. When we agreed to do the story with Jessica, we asked if she could make sure to keep the focus on Laney and her story. We were trying to help spark the memories of someone who may have known what happened to her. Jessica did a tremendous story that brought some attention to what we were doing, but especially to Laney and her unsolved murder.

The story ran on a Thursday night, if I remember correctly. The next day at school, many of my forensic science students had seen the story and began to ask questions.

Is that why you have all of those white boards in the back of the room?

What happened to her?

How did she get in the river?

When did she go missing?

Who have you talked to?

The questions kept coming. Whatever I had planned that day in class was lost pretty quickly. But I began to notice something. Students were all engaged and coming up with all sorts of questions. And it wasn't only the straight-A students asking the questions. It was students who I very rarely heard from unless I pulled it out of them. Many were looking things up on their computers and saying things like, "Hey, Mr. Hubbard, did you talk to this person?" Some began looking through social media posts to see if they could find anything. Calculating when Laney disappeared, some students deduced the age of her friends and the people involved in the case and stated most of the people we needed to talk to were probably on Facebook, because they were too old to know how to use the newer social media outlets. They were right!

This went on in my class for days. We didn't do anything I had planned to do for about two weeks because the kids were so involved in helping us out. It was something to behold. I have taught for three decades, and I'm not sure I have ever had a lesson that the students couldn't walk away from. It was like a virus. It was spreading to all of them, and they couldn't get over it. Many students decided they wanted to try to look at a case on their own. It was really exciting to watch as the students started talking to each other and then giving Evan and me ideas almost every day. Many we had already researched, but some were new, and we wanted to look into them. Something special was happening, but I wasn't quite sure yet what it was.

I was in that period of my career that many people go through in which you feel like you are going through the motions. This week, this lesson. Next week, that plan. Day by day, week by week, the same pattern, over and over again. Don't get me wrong, I was still teaching with excitement and loved being around the students; that's my personality. It was easy for me because Forensic Science is not a normal course in most high schools. As something they elected to take, the students were always excited to learn the application of all the other science classes they had taken prior to this class. It was a small, real-life example of the proverbial, "When am I going to ever use this?" question many students ask while in school. But what Evan and I were experiencing was like nothing I have ever felt. Each day was different. Each phone call or social media search gave us a new perspective. There was something happening inside of me that I had not felt in a long time. It was that nervous, butterfly-filled stomach feeling I used to get before each football game I played in high school and college. I was excited!

Evan and I had created a bond that was different than most student/teacher relationships. His intelligence and pure inquisitive manner was refreshing, and he was teaching me about things like social media, internet searches, and so much more. It became a mutual respect between someone of Generation X, who often think we are smarter because of our experience, and Generation Z, who want to prove to you they are capable of difficult tasks without your help. Evan was open to my ideas, and I was open to his. He had some great insight and also respect for my experience. If I had not met Evan at the time that I did, Laney's case files may never have gotten pulled out from the dark room those boxes had been sitting in for so long.

The more we worked on her case, the more I felt there was something else that needed to be done. It was eating at me day and night. My wife thought I was spending too much time obsessing over this, but she knew it wasn't going to go away any time soon. I don't usually get stuck on something to the point of annoyance, but I couldn't shake the feeling I wasn't doing enough, that something was missing.

What am I doing?

Why am I so caught up in this?

Why can't I sleep at night?

What is going on?

Then it hit me. It was if Laney herself tapped me on the shoulder and pointed to the many whiteboards, pictures, and names all over my room. As I stared deeply into the picture we'd taken on one of our adventures of the smooth waters of the Ohio River where Laney's body was found, it came to me. Laney wasn't only calling us to look at her case; she had a greater plan. I truly felt a sudden heavy heart for all of the families who had lost a loved one to murder. It was as if the picture of the wide riverbend was saying, "There are more." There are more stories of tragedy that have been lost. There are more families who want to know someone cares. As I said earlier in the book, I had begun to look at my faith a bit more during this journey, and I was wondering whether Laney was speaking for others standing next to her in Heaven who needed a voice to tell what happened to them.

Was Laney speaking to me as an angel, telling me there were more?

Was she showing me all the work we had put in and the lessons we had learned?

Was she saying we could do more by having others do the work for those families still grieving?

Was she telling me I was in a perfect place to provide valuable learning experiences for my students and help speak for those who could not?

I started to reflect on those two weeks of going off script in my class. The students were becoming like Evan and me. It wasn't about looking into the psychology of serial killers like Ted Bundy or John Wayne Gacy. It wasn't about giving attention to the killers, which oftentimes steals the stories of the victims. It was about Laney. It was about Laney as a beautiful young woman who was taken from us too early. Many of the students' eyes filled with tears as they spoke about what happened to her. Then one student asked, "How many cold cases are there?" At the time, I had no idea, so I told them to look it up. The number was staggering, and the students couldn't believe that so many killers have gotten away with murder and the families of the victims have no answers.

At that moment, in a calm, quiet voice, I said to Evan, "What do you think about a class here at Mason High School for students to experience the gratification of doing work like this for other families?" At first, Evan looked at me, a bit perplexed, but then he responded with, "I think that is a great idea!" The wheels starting turning, then we both started spouting ideas at once: This is what we can do. This is how students will learn from this. This is going to be a challenge, but what is life without challenge? I had to write a curriculum and a proposal to get the class okayed by our administration and the board of education, but I couldn't do it alone. Evan, as a junior in high school, sat right next to me as we researched any other programs doing something like this. We scoured articles to see if anyone had experience with organizing something such as a class for high school students to dive into real cases. We found a couple of college programs, but even those were clubs or organizations outside the normal classroom experience. We realized we may be the first to do something like this. Wow! Talk about blindly diving in headfirst! I hoped we wouldn't screw this up.

In our search, we found the Cold Case Research Institute founded by Sheryl "Mac" McCullom, an award-winning CSI from Atlanta, Georgia, and renowned true crime author. She has been in the field for a long time and is seen as one of the best to ever do this work. I looked at Evan and said, "Maybe she can help us." I was a bit nervous to call. One, she might not respond at all, considering she is pretty famous and extremely busy; or two, she could think we were a bit crazy and not really serious about wanting to do this. One thing I learned while looking into Laney's case was just do it. What is the worst thing they can say to you? No. We had already gotten that from some people, but most had been pretty open to speak with us, so maybe Sheryl would as well.

We started with an email to introduce ourselves to give her a heads-up on what we were looking to accomplish. Thinking that would stay in her inbox for a while, we went on with our work on Laney's case. To my surprise, Sheryl emailed me that same night and replied with something like, "Well, honey, I'd be glad to talk to you." Anyone who knows Sheryl knows what I mean when she would say things like, "Well, honey." That's who she is. She is one of the kindest human beings I have ever come in contact with. That demeanor is natural and a bit hard to believe, considering the awful things she has seen day in and day out in her line of work. She couldn't wait to help us get this started.

To her, like many people I have spoken to who are in or have been in that field, it was an opportunity to shape a whole new generation of people interested in bringing light to cases that have fallen into the dark waters of a cold case. Her insight was invaluable. She listened to our ideas and gave us credit for the work we were doing on Laney's case and on bringing the cold case class idea to light. She gave us ideas of what to do and what kinds of things to avoid. Sheryl truly is a bright light in the dark world of cold cases. Without hesitation, she will text me back or call me to answer any questions we might have, and she was crucial in helping Evan and me develop the Cold Case MHS Program. She even took time out of her day to call my assistant principal, Shanna Bumiller, to ease her concerns about keeping the students safe while doing this work. Her kind words and her ability to emphasize the importance of the work these students could do was the turning point in putting all this into action.

We got the approval of the administration and the school board to move forward the next year with the first ever Cold Case MHS class. As we ventured into this new realm of learning, I told the students we were all in this together. I had no idea where this was going to go or how to get there, but we were going to do it together. The students broke up into groups. They searched cold case websites, attorneys general pages, podcasts, and news articles, trying to find a case that drew them in. We did exercises on reading critically. We talked to detectives in the area on how to gather information and how to organize our thoughts. We learned how to check people's backgrounds through public records and how to find their addresses or other contact information. Obviously the students were more social media aware than I was, but I had to learn fast to make sure we didn't reach out to the wrong people. We were collaborating, discussing, organizing, and learning from each other and from experts in the field. We were learning by doing. I really needed to help the students understand these were not research projects but life projects. It was about building rapport with those we would speak with. It was about reaching deep into your brain to figure out where to go to get answers to the questions about each victim and their case.

This class was also a chance for me as a teacher to instill something that all of us need to have when we encounter people around us: empathy. This is the one characteristic that is the hardest to build for each of us. Understanding what others are going through is so difficult to do without actually going through it yourself. As mentioned before, when Evan and I started on Laney's case, we did not have any idea what people around her were going through because we had not experienced it.

We learned quickly that it was much more than we expected. Once we saw the true emotions of the loss, it was no longer Laney's case; it was Laney's life. I knew I needed to show this to the students, so when they got into their cases they would understand feeling the loss of those closest to the victim. No matter what lifestyle, age, color, or gender, these victims were wives, daughters, sons, fathers, and friends to so many people, and people are grieving every day for their unfair, violent departure from Earth.

Laney's friends heard how we were using Laney as a model for our class and how we hoped to help as many people as we could, even if it was only to comfort them with the fact that someone still cares enough to try to bring their loved ones' stories back into the open. When I reached out to Laney friends to see if they would share their stories about her and how it has affected them over the years, at first they were not sure if it would be a good idea, but after some time to think about it, almost all of them agreed to share their stories with our class. In thirty-three years of teaching, I have never seen students so focused on a "lesson"—what her friends were saying about Laney, that night, and the pain they feel every day. Let's just say by the end of the discussion, there were not many dry eyes in the room. I had heard those stories, but it hit me as hard that time as it did the several times before. At that moment, the work to bring cold cases into the open was no longer merely a project. As they began to call people involved with their cases, I had never been more proud of my students as I was at that moment. They got it!

We are now six years into Cold Case MHS. Each year students never cease to amaze me on how much work they put into the lives of the victims of violent crimes. The emotional phone calls with families and friends, the organized interviews of detectives who worked or are currently working on the cases, and the tremendous, empathetic presentations given by the students at the end of the year to represent the victim with honor is something to behold.

It is heartwarming to watch the families of the victims who attend our presentations as they embrace our students at the end of the night and say, "Thank you." We have brought attention to forty cases since 2019, and in some of them we have sparked enough interest for law enforcement to at least review the case one more time. Our students have been recognized for their work by media outlets and by other schools across the United States. Several other schools have contacted me to ask how we did it and how they could do it as well. The students pretty much run the show, and I am merely the facilitator of their actions. Each year we try something new to allow the students to create valuable experiences and to further get the stories of the victims back into the spotlight.

We also produce a podcast called *Cold Case MHS* featuring our students and the projects they have worked so hard on. The students produce and edit, and even the theme songs have been sung by former or current students. Through Laney and her story, we have been able to allow students to excel in many areas, but the one that is the greatest to see is the development of their heart. It is not just a class anymore; it is a movement. A movement to get people involved in helping bring attention to those stories that seem to have been forgotten. At the end of each year, I congratulate the students for the work they have done and the hearts they have helped. Then I look on my classroom wall at the picture of Laney and say to her, "I hope this is what you wanted."

We will not stop on Laney's story, and I know deep in my soul that she brought us all together. She took an eager young man, introduced him to a teacher who needed a purpose, and opened our minds and hearts to the thousands of victims whose cases still linger in the dark. Just like in life, even in death, Laney's touch is still felt. Cold Case MHS would not exist without her and we would not be…

"Speaking for Those Who Cannot."

Faces of the Victims covered in Cold Case MHS since 2019

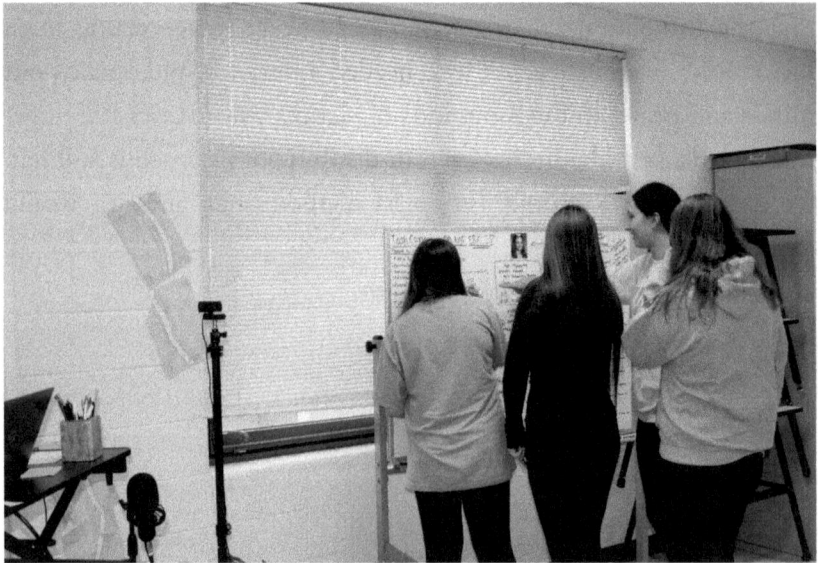

2024 Students working on Cold Case

Whiteboard work for current Cold Cases at MHS students

Montgomery County Sheriff Cold Case Detective speaks to Cold Case MHS students.

MHS history teacher listening and brainstorming with students on their case.

---

12

---

## Whispers From Beyond

---

**"Angels remind us that even in the midst of chaos, there is always a higher plan at work."**
— Neale Donald Walsch, "Conversations with God"

AS I PADDLED my kayak out into the middle of Thurman Lake, in McCormick, South Carolina, I tried to get to my cell phone to take a picture of the beautiful water and tree line that surrounded me. The small, rippling waves gently pushed my kayak up and down, giving me the sensation of rocking back and forth like that of a breezy day on a front porch swing. The only problem is I couldn't get that damn phone to work.

"Memory is full. Manage your memory by going to your settings."

"Damn it!" I tried to delete some old photos, but the glare of the sun on my screen was blinding, and I couldn't see what I was doing. I know I deleted some photos, so that had to work, right?

"Memory is full. Manage your memory by going to your settings."

"Seriously! What the...?" As I fiddled with that stupid phone, the wind kept me moving through the water. Before I knew it, I had drifted all the way out into the middle of the lake. I looked up to realize I was the only one out on the lake, and the beauty was tremendous. It was truly the picture I was trying to capture on my phone. At that moment, it hit me. I wasn't supposed to take a picture of it to send to my family or post on social media. I was supposed to sit in the vast, lonely lake to simply take it in. God was telling me to relax, enjoy, and embrace all of Earth's beauty. The sun warmed my skin, but it also seemed to warm my soul. The distorted mirror image of the trees in the water brought a calm to me that was indescribable. I sat in that kayak for nearly two hours, every once in a while paddling to a different location to change my perspective of the lake. Each time, the immense beauty was overwhelming.

It was a moment of reflection. It was time I needed to refocus on the things that were important. It was a time to be thankful for all the good fortune I have had in my life. It was a time to reflect on the journey I have been on since looking into Laney and her case and how it has changed me. It was a time to be thankful for the people Laney has brought into my life. It was a time to give thought to the path she has pushed me on and the many lives Evan and I have affected since that day we decided to look into a cold case.

In the previous chapters, I spoke of the resurgence of my faithful journey.

Was there a greater being directing my life and the lives of others?

Were there signs that came from above, that led me to Evan, and to Laney's case? Did Laney reach out to me to say there are so many other people who need attention brought to their stories? I don't know. It seemed a bit miraculous to think that looking up one person's tragic story would connect me to a greater cause like it had. The lessons learned, the communication with people, and the true sense of purpose were overtaking my every thought. There was so much more we could do, and who better to do it than students with natural curiosity and the will to do something good for the world?

After Cold Case MHS was born, we had to nurture the program through the years in the hopes that one day the work we were doing would possibly bring justice to at least one family that has suffered such tragedy. Losing a loved one to violent crime and not getting the answer to why, or at least who, is an agony that seems so unfair to those still living.

As we started to reach out to family and friends of lost loved ones, each time as we listened to their heartbreak and to their hunger for someone to care enough to look one more time, it became more real. The victims come from many different back-grounds, from loving mothers who seemed to have had no enemies to young children who had no way to stop the awful outcome that would take them from us too soon. Many seemed to have no worries in the world, while for others, the worries took them into a lifestyle they could not escape. Some most likely succumbed to the violence of someone close to them, while others seemed to be in the wrong place at the wrong time. One thing they all had in common was that they did not deserve what happened to them. Their memo-ries to most of the public have been erased by time, but to those who loved them, it is a day-to-day fight. It is a memory of the moment they heard the news or saw the victim that haunts them until the day they reunite with them in Heaven. Some families had to suffer other losses due to the overwhelming stress placed on mothers, fathers, sisters, brothers, or siblings who could not stop the search for answers that would not come.

Over the six years of its existence, Cold Case MHS has tried to find some small bits of information that could help police departments reevaluate or reopen cases that seemed to have gone dormant. In almost all of them the response from the families has been tremendous. Many family members have been brought to tears because someone cares about their loved ones. I cannot imagine the loneliness felt by families as the cases go year by year with no new information or leads. I would say that some are surprised and a bit skeptical when they receive a phone call from a teacher and several students to talk about the murder of their relative. Many look us up online to confirm who we are and to check to see what our purpose really is. I don't blame them, because we have found from talking with many families that sick individuals will call them to say they have information, try to scam them by saying they have information, or even some despicable slimes will call and harass the family to get a reaction from them. We often have to spend a few days allowing them to ask us questions so they know what we are trying to do. What a great learning experience this is for our students. This makes our students realize this is so much more than a research project. As I keep telling them, it is a Human Project.

As we have progressed in the last six years, the relationships built with family members is something that is so difficult to describe. The connection through tragedy often lends itself to friendships you never thought you would have. For me, it has been a blessing to be able to speak with individuals who would most likely never cross my path, but the real blessing is how we stay connected even if it is only to throw out a "How ya doing?" text every once in a while. Many of them tell me about their families, their work, or how their day is going. Others will take a few days to respond, but eventually they do. Almost all will, at some point, say, "Thank you!"

When doing this type of work, you often find stories and people that stick in your mind. It may be because of how nice they were to you. It may be because of how tragic the story was. Or it may be because it's hard to believe it is still unsolved. In all of them, there is something that touches me that I can't let go.

In the next section, I will tell you about some of the stories that are too hard to put in the file cabinet. At the end of the book, I will also list the names, with pictures, of all the victims, with a brief summary of each, that Cold Case MHS has tried to bring back to light. We are trying to play a small part in a huge problem, not only in Ohio, but around the country.

The picture used in the posters of Angela Marie Steele shows a gorgeous woman, her sweater slightly off her shoulder, with long brown hair, and a heartwarming smile. She was the mother of two wonderful girls. She was the epitome of the small town beauty that the men of that town would fall all over themselves to get to know. She loved her kids with all her heart. She would take them on picnics or to town to go play on the playground. In a conversation with Megan, her oldest daughter, she told me Angela was the best mom a girl could have. At the tender age of eight, that is exactly what Megan needed. Megan was in a new town, going to a new school, and wasn't sure how she fit in. Angela was there to assure her that everything was going to be okay.

The family had moved from a neighboring town to a rural area between Marseilles, Ohio, and Kenton, Ohio. The area resembles a green-and-brown checkerboard of farm fields as far as you can see. The vast space between homes and towns is what you imagine the area around Mayberry to be. The rural roads are small and most likely not well lit at night, so images of monsters crawling out of the corn fields could also fill your imagination. It was the kind of place that would be easy to hide family issues. Megan, Angela's oldest daughter, was not happy about the move. The house they bought was a farmhouse in the middle of nowhere, and they didn't even farm. One thing she noticed was that her mom didn't appear as happy living so far from civilization, and it was causing friction in her mom and stepfather's marriage. The fighting grew more intense over time, but Angela stuck around for the sake of her daughters.

Knowing they needed money, Angela would drive the eleven or twelve miles to Kenton, Ohio, to work a late-night shift at a local sports bar. She would often close for the owner, causing her to arrive home sometimes as late as two a.m. Megan noticed her mother's late-night arrivals as Angela would make her way to the master bedroom that Megan could hear from her room through the open doors. Each morning, Megan could see her mother sleeping as her stepfather tried to get Megan and her little sister ready for school. On June 4, 1999, Megan felt weird when she was getting ready for school and her mother was not in bed. She always looked at her mother's peaceful, sleeping face before heading off to the bus stop. But that day was different.

*Where's Mom?* was whispering in her mind.

While viewing the rural landscape through the truck window, Megan was focused on the uneasiness that was brewing in her stomach. Why was her mother not home? The ride to the bus stop was far away, according to the measurements of an eight year old, but something wasn't right. Megan had a very strong bond with her mother that often transcended physical presence. She had been with her by herself for many years before Angela married her second husband, Megan's current stepfather. Megan had a feeling something was wrong.

Suddenly, her wandering mind was jarred by the abrupt stop of her stepfather's truck near a car that had been completely burned, almost to its frame. Megan had trouble seeing what was going on, but her stepfather hurried back to the truck, backed out, then proceeded to quickly drive Megan home. It didn't appear that Megan was going to school that day, but why?

The day then became a blur. Family members started showing up to the house. They seemed concerned and saddened by something, but Megan wasn't sure what was happening. Then she looked into Angela's room, and she still wasn't there. Something was very wrong. Shortly after Megan's grandparents, Angela's parents, had arrived, she was packing a bag, getting into the car with them, and leaving, never to return to that house again. What was going on?

On that fateful morning, the car that was burned on the side of the road was Angela Marie Steele's. At an initial glance, it appeared as if the car had run head-on into a tree on the side of the road. Further investigation would tell another story. The car would have had to have made an exact ninety-degree-angle turn off the road to be situated up against the tree perpendicular to the road. The front end of the car barely had a dent, indicating it had not hit the tree at high speed. As police scoured the scene, it would later be determined that there was the body of a female in the passenger seat of the vehicle. The identity of the body would later be confirmed as that of the beautiful mother of two, Angela Marie Steele, and the cause of the car fire would be ruled an arson. It was evident the crime scene had been staged. Angela had been murdered, and the fire was to cover up any evidence that may have been left behind.

Megan's uneasiness had foreshadowed what was to come on that truck ride to the bus stop. Her mother was gone, and her family dynamic would change forever. After her mother's death, Megan rarely saw the stepfather or half-sister she had been living with. She left in her grandparents' car that morning, never to return. She watched her grandparents dwindle into depression that would take their lives way too early. Megan and her half-sister had to grow up without their wonderful mother. Taking its toll on both of them, it would prove difficult to adjust to life without her. Through years of heartache, the pain caused both girls to fall into detrimental behaviors that would take a long time to overcome. After twenty-five years, they seem to have fought off their demons to lead very productive lives, but in talking with Megan, you can still feel the agony she goes through each day.

Like every murder involving a spouse, Angela's husband would become a prime person of interest in her case. It was he who called the police, but only after he had called his parents first when he arrived back home. Angela's car happened to be on his route to take Megan to the bus stop in a rural county with hundreds of backroads to travel. To hit that particular tree where her car was found would have been in the opposite direction of where she would have driven home from her job in Kenton. According to some information we gathered from friends, a rumor had started that the stepfather had the smell of gasoline on him when the police arrived, and he stated that he had been cutting the grass. This statement has not been verified, so let's call this hearsay. Other friends mentioned Angela complaining about abuse and that she'd had enough.

It had been rumored that, on June 5th, after picking the girls up from school, Angela was going to take the girls and leave town. Again, this information cannot be completely verified, and, unfortunately, we will never know the truth about these rumors. Her husband, by simply being her husband, is a logical person of interest, but we do not have any proof of his connection to her crime. Angela's case has gone cold for twenty-five years with no new evidence or movement on it.

Could there be other persons of interest for her murder? Yes.

The case, at a glance, is intriguing but not much different than many cases in the state of Ohio in which leads have seemed to run out. But there were some things that really drew me to spend some extra time on Angela's case after the students had completed their year of research. The biggest was Megan. Megan is a wonderful person to talk with. She is kind, warm-hearted, and genuine. She truly expressed her gratitude for what we were doing and did everything she could to help us. Megan and I still keep in contact, sometimes merely to say "hello" or see how our families are doing.

In our deep dives into these cases, we talk about finding out who the victim was as a person before their fateful end. In our quest to know more about Angela, Megan sent us some pictures. Some of the pictures were glamor shot quality, showing the pure beauty of a woman; and others were pictures of a loving mother with both daughters smothered by her nurturing hugs. One image reached deep into my soul. It had Angela sitting with her beautiful daughters in her lap. The angelic photo was a foreshadowing of what would happen to her only one week later. This was the last photo taken of Angela with her daughters, and it brought a calm but eerie feeling to my students and me. It was as if someone knew she was going to be called home to her maker very soon.

EVERY CASE WE HAVE LOOKED INTO IS DIFFERENT YET IN SO many ways the same. The victim is someone who didn't deserve to die, and in many cases, their death didn't make sense. Each one touches your heart in a different way but always hits deep into your soul, leaving the question of "Why?"

Why that person?

Why that time?

Why that tragedy?

Our cases have taken us on a virtual journey from small-town Ohio to the metropolis of Cincinnati to towns and cities in between. Some places seem so quaint that things like murder don't seem possible, while others the cases become a data point in a cluster full of evil events. All communities, big, small, rich, or poor, have dark secrets that are hard to imagine. Springfield, Ohio, is no exception to these ugly truths.

Actually, Springfield is a moderately sized community, but its violent crime numbers are staggering. There is almost a distinct line between safety and danger in that town. On one side is a quiet, small college town, while the other side seems to be riddled with the bullets of a violent past and a very scary future.

As an educator, I have been able to teach and coach in both sides of the spectrum mentioned in the previous paragraph. The one thing that is consistent is that kids are kids, and where they come from and what they have or don't have does not always determine where they will end up. Some of the greatest stories are of those students who grow up to use their experience as a youth to better the community in which they live. Many of those young people feel the loyalty to the communities they grew up in and want to pay their success forward to others living there currently. It may take these individuals many years to mature enough to realize their behaviors, both good or bad, are witnessed by those around them, including young individuals they see every day.

Many will go through a rough life of bad decisions leading to bad outcomes but somewhere along the way see the impact it has had on those who look up to them. It could be a near-death experience or divine intervention that wakes them up, but eventually they realize they could be so much more productive if they would lead in a positive light rather than the darkness they had been traveling for some time.

CHRISTOPHER DEARMOND WAS ONE SUCH YOUNG MAN. HE was an outstanding athlete at Springfield North High School. He was a standout basketball player with tremendous potential to go to the next level. He was tall with a great physique and that natural ability to make people aware of his athletic prowess. Unfortunately, Chris also had a short fuse and didn't respond to authority very well. He grew up in a rough part of Springfield with many negative influences around him. Many of them were not great for an impressionable young man looking to fit in. He had a head full of hair and let it grow to a good length, but his high school basketball coach didn't believe in that type of self-expression. He was a strict man with rules that included short haircuts to show respect and loyalty to discipline. Chris was not exactly one to follow the rules, and his hair was his "chick magnet." He was a handsome young man, and to him the hair was part of the reason.

Chris decided the rules were not for him, so he transferred to the other high school in the district, Springfield South High School. He went on to finish a pretty successful career at South, but outside influences changed his trajectory as an athlete. Like many young men who seem to have a way with the ladies, he made a few life-changing decisions. He started having children at a very young age. He now had the responsibility for others and had to try to do his best to make ends meet. This sometimes leads to bad decisions for a young man surrounded by a volatile environment, but those decisions did not define who he was. He was a loving man with children to bring up, and one day he realized there were little eyes watching his every move. Chris decided he had to grow up. He had to set a good example, not only for his kids, but for all of the other kids in the community.

Chris always cut his friends' hair growing up, which was ironic, considering his long hair was the reason to transfer schools. It hit him that he had a talent, and he could use that talent for good. He worked hard at a barbershop trying to pay his dues and get enough money to pursue his certificate from an accredited barber school. It took him many years to accomplish that goal, but he never gave up.

The day he received his certificate, he could not wait to show it off to his family. His children, many of them grown by then, were so proud of him for his sheer determination to complete what he had started. He was an inspiration to them and to those in his community. He wanted to give back to those who had supported him and to those who needed a role model to look up to. He had grown up with little money and knew what many of the young people of Springfield were going through, so he would offer free haircuts to those who couldn't pay. He used that time to disperse wisdom of his life—his experiences, mistakes, and dreams—to those young people in Springfield who needed that push to make better decisions. He became a community leader, speaking at churches, town meetings, and sometimes on the corner of the street, trying to bring peace to an area that had seen its share of unrest for a really long time.

On March 17, 2012, around 9:54 a.m., the world would change for Chris' family and the town he had loved so much. He always arrived early to open the barbershop and get ready for the day. Many in the community knew he would be there because he often gave free haircuts before the shop was officially open. He was on the phone with a woman he had been dating, and he was happy and excited about the day. Suddenly, the mood changed. The girl-friend heard him say, "Hold on. Who is that?" Shots rang out! He told his girlfriend he had been shot and to call the police. When the police arrived, they found Chris lying in the middle of the shop with multiple gunshot wounds. He was airlifted to a local hospital but did not survive his injuries.

The girlfriend, right after calling the police, ran to tell his daughter India, who worked in the same building, that her father had been shot and the police were on their way to the scene. India immediately called her father, but the phone went to voicemail. She tried again, but it went to voicemail again. India called her uncle,

Chris' brother. He tried calling Chris, too. This time Chris answered, told him he wasn't going to make it and to not tell his kids what had happened. Even while he was dying, Chris was thinking about his kids. He didn't want his kids to hear him at that time. He wanted them to remember him happy and joking around. India says to this day that her father did not answer the phone call from her because he didn't want her to have that as her last memory of him. She said the outpouring of support during that time from the community was tremendous. She knew that someone knew something, but they were too afraid to tell.

Who would want to kill a community leader like Chris? A man who came from very little to being someone almost everyone looked up to?

As we talked to family, friends, and anyone we could find who knew him, we began to get a picture of who Chris was and the turmoil going on in the area. In our podcast episode, "The Long Dispute," we discuss the long-running feud between two families in that area of Springfield. Unfortunately, some of the younger individuals in the rival families did not always listen to the wisdom given by their elders, like Chris. Territories were established and defended. Fights were common and retaliation was almost guaranteed for any wrong done to the other. In a series of events, several confrontations had occurred. Fists were thrown and bullets were shot. Chris, being the calm voice of the city in turmoil, tried to step in to stop the violence. In doing so, a rival family member felt he had been disrespected in front of his peers. That was something that could not happen, and actions had to be taken. The following day, Chris was taken out to make a statement.

Through the years, rumors flew through the community about who was responsible for this tragic action. India, Chris' daughter, told us she knew who did it, and he even admitted it, but the police could not completely connect him to the crime. The killer stood far enough away in the small barbershop to deliver the fatal shots but not leave any evidence behind. They slipped out the door before anyone else could see them and melted into the nearby neighborhood without a trace. To this day, Chris' killer has not been charged, but he may have put himself in a situation he cannot get out of this time.

This particular case rang deep with me because my oldest daughter went to Wittenberg University, a college on the west side of Springfield. If I had known the statistics about Springfield, I may not have let her go there. I'm glad I didn't because she flourished there and has gone on to do some great things in her life.

The other reason this stuck with me was India. India has been a tremendous resource for information about her father's case, but most of all she has been a genuine person throughout our conversations. She is kind, strong, and as determined as her father. We still exchange pleasantries from time to time. She is a true role model for those around her. She has gone back to school, like her father, to beat the odds and become a nurse. She works in the emergency trauma department and is continuing her education to do more. India is not only a role model for those close to her, but she is a role model to me. Her determination is infectious, and it makes me want to make sure we can get her father's story out there again, in the hopes that someone will come forward with information that leads to the killer's conviction.

I also cannot let go of what happened to India and her siblings while we were looking into Chris' case. At the end of our semester, our students do a livestream public presentation of their findings from the year. I texted India to ask her for any pictures she would like us to display and asked her to send us any fun or uplifting stories about her father she wanted us to use in the presentation. The text I received back sent a shock through the students who had been talking to her for many months—and me: "Hello. Sorry, can you give me until later to send those to you? My mother was just shot and killed by the SAME person today."

WHAT?

I didn't know what to say. I told the students what she said and we stood there in silence. Tears began to form in all our eyes because we had become so attached to India and two of her sisters, and we could not believe it. I responded with, "Oh my God! I have no words to express our deepest sympathies and please do not worry about sending us those pictures. You go take care of your family." Thinking that would be the end of our conversation for a while, I did not expect to get another text the very next day with not only photos of her father, but also her mother. We now had another story to tell about this long dispute that has continued for another eleven years and cost the life of another wonderful human being. This time the culprit was caught through the use of a RING camera and is awaiting trial for the murder of India's mother, Racquel Flowers, on February 5, 2023.

∼

THESE TYPES OF INTERACTIONS WOULD GO ON FOR THE NEXT six years after we started working on Laney's case and others. More people each year were being added to my list of people I would grow to admire. I admire their drive to never let go of the story of their loved ones. I admire their resolve to keep fighting to find the truth. I admire their ability to carry on the legacy of their loved ones through their own actions by bettering their own lives and honoring their loved ones as they succeed in life. From Shauntay, the cousin of a wonderful mother; Alicia Jackson, who was brutally slain in her living room with her two-year-old son sitting in his highchair right next to her; to Donald Branham, the father of a nine-year-old daughter who was killed, then left to burn in an arson attempt on the home in which she was living. From the grand-daughter of Harry W. Smith or Mr. Walmart, as he was warmly known, who was attacked in his rural home before going to church, all for a little small change and some sentimental articles. To Paula, the friend of Stacey Colbert, who went missing from her apartment only to have her remains discovered several years later in the woods by a hunter. I admire their determination to keep the story of their beloved friend, daughter, grandfather, or cousin in the spotlight even as it seems the light is dimming.

There are many more stories of connections I could go on writing about, but it might take a whole book of its own to cover them all. Laney reached down to me to take my hand and guide me to all of the people I have met and become friends with over these six years, and the people I will meet in the future as we continue this project. Like whispers from beyond, she quietly spoke to me of those who still have a story to tell, in the hope that one day their loved ones will be able to finally rest in peace.

# 13

# Unanswered Prayers

**"Some unanswered prayers are only because God doesn't want to do something for us. He wants to do something through us."**
— Bill Johnson

ON DECEMBER 10, 1997, life would instantly change forever for so many people. A beautiful young woman would walk outside a bowling alley by herself, never to be seen alive again. The days following would test the faith of those close to her. Prayers were flowing nonstop both in private and in public. Those who knew her and even those who didn't were asking God to bring her home. As the days passed, those prayers went unanswered. Until, unfortunately, the answers to their prayers were not what they expected. Alana "Laney" Gwinner did finally come home, both to West Chester, Ohio, and to her maker. At least they knew where she was. She wasn't freezing in the cold weather of Ohio in January. She wasn't being held against her will. She wasn't being tortured or abused. But she was no longer alive. The prayers to find Laney had been answered, but the prayers to find her well and in good health were not. The questions toward God were many.

Why would he let something so bad happen to such a beautiful person?

Why would he take someone so young with so much potential?

Those answers will go unanswered for eternity, but those with faith believe that God always has a plan. We may not know the plan. We may not understand the plan. We certainly don't always like the plan. But most accept the idea that God has a plan.

Like the sunshine coming through the clouds after a hurricane, light does break through the darkness of tragedy. The rebuilding begins. The memories of the heartbreak will never go away, but they can be the motivation to keep moving forward. For Laney's family and friends, time stood still for a period. Disbelief that something so devastating could happen to someone so close to them paralyzed them for days, weeks, months, and for some it would take years to dig themselves out of the thick mud that clogged their souls.

The memories of Laney would soon drive those close to her to keep pushing for answers. They set up vigils. They spoke to the press. They hovered over the police departments to spur them along, until they could find who did this. Unfortunately, time became the enemy. The longer the case went on, the less pushing people could do. Life, although it sounds harsh, does go on. Friends started their own families. Reporters found new stories. Police had more cases to investigate. As stated in Chapter 5, time also took its toll on the family. Alana Gwinner's case and story went cold. Every few years, another news story would highlight her case, but only those who knew her truly understood what the real story was. Friends kept an eye on the "Justice for Alana 'Laney' Gwinner" Facebook page to see if any new posts showed up or they would post their "happy birthdays" to her each year. Unfortunately, those posts slowed down as well, but Laney's friends and family continue to hold on to hope that one day she will be able to rest knowing who committed that awful act of murder.

Maybe that was the plan. Maybe she couldn't have been saved that night and the plan changed. Through people who held on to hope and those affected many years later by her story, the search for the truth in Laney's case has brought much-needed attention to other families going through similar fights for justice. One day Laney's case will be solved; until then, I believe Laney had a bigger idea. Like in life, the picture was bigger than her. She continues to reach out to people like Frank Smith, the retired Butler County Sheriff's Detective. He spent his last few years on the force doing everything he could to bring justice to Laney. Do I think he may have found the killer? I think he may have, but the evidence just isn't there for an arrest and, ultimately, a conviction. Laney reached out to LaDonna Humphrey when she compared Laney's case with that of Melissa Witt's. Laney reached out to Evan and me at the right time so that we could continue what others had started. She's not gone. Her memories are still strong, and her presence is still felt, but it seems she wanted us to help search for answers to many other tragic stories of those lost to violent crimes.

All it will take to solve Laney's case is persistence. That one detective who won't let it go. That one person to keep pushing to find something that will turn the case around. The public who hears the story and comes forward with any information that may lead to a clue. It can be done and I, along with others I have drawn into the case, will keep going until I find something. Cases like these are being solved every day because someone will not stop. Like the case of Marcia King, known as the "Buck Skin" girl for almost thirty-five years.

A young Detective Hickey, from the Miami County Sheriff's Office, could not believe she was still a "Jane Doe" when he started working on her case. It had been thirty-five years, and her loved ones had no idea she had been murdered. She wasn't from Ohio when she was killed in 1981, and finding her relatives would prove to be a daunting task. Detective Hickey could not stand that her name was still the "Buck Skin" girl, because of the jacket she was wearing when she was found. He had to figure out who she was. Through unique thought processes and new technology, Detective Hickey went on a mission to find her true identity. He heard of a new technique called genetic genealogy that was being used in some cases across the country. A team of scientists and detectives worked hard to figure out who she was. The new technology got its recognition through the "Golden State Killer" case, but Detective Hickey's team was using it at the same time. Through pollen and water mineral data, his team was able to track her whereabouts for several years and, on the day after the "Golden State Killer" was identified, genetic genealogy revealed the "Buck Skin" girl to be Marcia King. Marcia was a drifter with mental health issues, often hitchhiking to different places around the country. Unfortunately, she took her last ride in Troy, Ohio, where she was found lying face down in a ditch next to a cornfield. To this day, her killer has not been identified, but sources tell me that may change very soon.

These stories continue to come out every day. The case of Sheryl Thompson who was kidnapped, raped, murdered, and left on the banks of the Little Miami River in 1978 was recently solved because Loveland Police Detective Steve Moster would not let it go. It turns out her murderer was most likely a serial killer that killed the likes of three other young ladies: Victoria Hincher in 1976, Nancy Theobald in 1977, and Charmaine Stolla in 1978.

Persistence in the murder case of Katelyn Markham, from Fairfield, Ohio, in 2011, led to the conviction of her fiancé John Carter.

The "I won't stop" attitude of Detective John Thompson of the

Franklin County Sheriff's Department near Columbus, Ohio, will soon most likely find the killer of Amy Hooper, brutally killed in her apartment in 1992.

These cases all have one thing in common, "Persistence." Keep going when it doesn't seem possible. There is a clue somewhere. Just keep looking.

That is what we plan to do for Laney. Keep going. Keep looking. Keep the pressure on. I hope someone in the Fairfield Police Department or the Butler County Sheriff's Office has that attitude, too. I believe there is someone there who will step up when the time comes. I know someone there won't be able to "let it go."

Unfortunately, when you read a book about a cold case, there is no ending. Laney has passed, but her memories and her reach has not. She has guided me to keep pushing, not only on her case, but on so many that have slipped into that dark file cabinet. One day Alana "Laney" Gwinner will be able to look down upon Earth and say "thank you" to someone for not giving up.

Until then, we keep praying for answers to those unanswered prayers.

14

# Letter to the Killer

"*No doubt I now grew very pale;—but I talked more fluently, and with a heightened voice. Yet the sound increased—and what could I do? It was a low, dull, quick sound—much such a sound as a watch makes when enveloped in cotton. I gasped for breath—and yet the officers heard it not. I talked more quickly—more vehemently; but the noise steadily increased. I arose and argued about trifles, in a high key, and with violent gesticulations; but the noise steadily increased. Why would they not be gone? I paced the floor to and fro with heavy strides as if excited to fury by the observations of the men—but the noise steadily increased. Oh God! What could I do? I foamed—I raved—I swore! I swung the chair upon which I had been sitting, and grated it upon the boards, but the noise arose overall and continually increased. It grew louder—louder—louder. And still, the men chatted pleasantly and smiled. Was it possible they heard not? Almighty God!—no, no! They heard!—they suspected!—they knew!—they were making a mockery of my horror! —this I thought, and this I think. But anything was better than this agony! Anything was more tolerable than this derision! I could bear those hypocritical smiles no longer! I felt that I must scream or die! and now—again!—hark! louder! louder! louder! Louder!"*

— Edgar Allen Poe, "The Tell-Tale Heart"

MR. KILLER,

I know you feel that you have gotten away with murder. You have slipped into the darkness for nearly twenty-six years. Every so often, the story of Laney's disappearance creeps its way back into the news, yet you somehow stay hidden. No matter how many times her life is beautifully described, there is always that one dark secret that ruins the ending. Her ending should have come after a long life with the joys of having a family, watching her kids grow up, and holding on to her loved ones into her golden years. At the end of an elderly person's journey in life, we all gather to remember the many years of joy, heartbreak, and proud moments we experienced with them. We tell jokes, we cry, but we all know that after seven or eight decades of life, their time has come. We all are better for knowing them, and we wish them well as they enter the gates of Heaven. In our hearts, we know the impact they have had on many lives and the many dreams they accomplished along the way.

These are what you have taken from those who knew and loved Laney.

She did have people cry and tell jokes about her at her funeral, but the difference was the dreams and accomplishments that would never come to be. You stole that from her, her family, and her friends. Your one bad decision destroyed decades of joy in a flash. In that dark moment, you extinguished a bright flame of hope.

I don't know exactly who you are yet, but I do feel you are still close. I have many questions to ask you. I know you think the truth won't come out because it has been hidden for so long, but can you tell me what it feels like to always be looking over your shoulder? You have to be saying to yourself, "Does anyone know what I did?" If you have confided in someone, do you trust them? Do you think they can keep that secret forever? For your sake, you better hope they don't have a conscience, either. Do you ever wonder what your life would be if you didn't commit murder? Do you ever wonder what Laney's life would be if you didn't kill her? I truly believe you will slip up and the police will one day walk through your door to take you to where you belong. You may be an old man by that time, but it's coming. If it doesn't happen in this life, you will be judged in the next.

Laney's murder wasn't like most involving a beautiful young woman taken in the dark. In a majority of those cases, there is a sexual component that causes the sick individual to pick the victim and do the awful things these people do to women.

You were different.

I don't think you were that type of monster. I'm giving you the benefit of the doubt and saying I don't believe you actually meant to kill Laney. Do I know what you were planning to do with her before her death? No. Could it have been a sick moment in your life that got out of hand? Yes, it definitely could be that, but giving you a little sympathy on that could be a waste. If you didn't mean to do it, then it has to be killing you inside. There is no way you cannot have that memory flash back into your mind over and over again. Does it come out at night? Do you randomly see her face while driving to work? I bet you haven't been back to a bowling alley since that night, because if you have, it has to be so hard to hold in your emotions. There has to be a ringing in your ears that keeps getting louder and louder. Medication doesn't help, does it? It's eating at you day by day. You are a good actor right now because you have practiced during all of these years, but it's getting harder, isn't it?

I'm sure the police have already spoken with you. As a matter of fact, I believe this happened shortly after Laney went missing, and I believe they talked to you again several years later. I bet you were nervous. I bet your anxious laugh made you feel like they knew something. I bet they could hear it in your voice. I know they haven't forgotten those conversations. I bet it's getting harder to breathe. I bet your chest hurts and you will let go and let it all out one day because it will have become too much.

Laney was beautiful, and you thought you had a chance with her. If only you could get her away from that guy she was with, she would see that you were her man. You tried to approach her at the bar or make a comment to her while she ordered her drinks. She didn't respond the first time, did she? Did that make you mad? I bet it did. You kept an eye on her and waited for her to come back by, because this time you had the line she couldn't resist. What did she do? Tell you to "FUCK off!" or something like that? Did it make you so angry you had to go outside to smoke or to cool off? While you were there, you saw her come out, didn't you? She was by herself, and you thought you could handle her. The problem was she wouldn't let you, would she? Things got out of hand. How did you subdue her? Did you hit her? Did you squeeze her too tight? How did it happen? The problem was that she stopped responding, didn't she? Oh shit! Now you had a problem. Did you panic, asshole? You did! You had to act fast.

You thought the river would hide your secrets forever. You thought whatever went into the waters would stay there. You probably know some things about the river and its power. But guess what? The river decided Laney needed to be found. It got crazy again for you after she was found, didn't it? You thought that by leaving town for a while everyone would forget, didn't you? Guess what? No one has forgotten. Somehow you have been able to hide, but it won't be forever. Someone will know something you thought they would never know. Someone saw you or helped you, and their conscience is wearing on their heart. It will all come out someday. I know that ringing in your head is actually the "Tell-Tale Heart" of Laney. It's getting louder and louder. You won't be able to take it much longer. They're coming for you.

Keep looking over your shoulder. The truth is there, and it won't be long before everyone knows it. The walls are closing in, Mr. Killer, and they are closing fast. You think because you have been hiding right out in the open for so long no one will ever know your true identity. Believe me, those who knew her have not forgotten what you did, and those of us new to the search are driven more than ever to unmask you. If it takes another twenty-five years of nipping at your heels, then that is what we will do. One day, that silence will become deafening. The ringing in your ears will get higher in pitch. It will drive you crazy. With each knock on the door, you will jump, thinking, as Poe said, that "anything is better than this agony!" Until, one day, it will sound like thunder cracking right above your head.

Sincerely,


RANDY

# 15

# "Dear Laney"

Mark 1:5: *And there went out unto him all the land of Judaea, and they of Jerusalem, and were all baptized of him in the river of Jordan, confessing their sins.*

Mark 1:8: *I indeed have baptized you with water: but he shall baptize you with the Holy Ghost.*

Mark 1:10: *And straightway coming up out of the water, he saw the heavens opened, and the Spirit like a dove descending upon him.*

DEAR LANEY,

I don't know what drew me to your life and, unfortunately, to your death, but I don't believe it was fate. I am a strong believer that things happen for a reason. I could have looked into nearly three thousand other cases in Ohio, but I found my way to yours through Fort Smith, Arkansas, nearly 780 miles away, all while sitting less than fourteen miles from the location of your last care-free night. My friend and colleague, LaDonna Humphrey, who I also believe was chosen for a reason, made a connection between you and the awful death of Melissa Witt. In my heart, I believe it was meant to be this way. I don't know if you and Melissa have met up there in Heaven and talked about those of us still here on Earth and decided, "Hey, these two look like the right ones." Or perhaps is it pure luck that all of our paths have crossed? I don't think so. It was fate. I know that I was meant to read that Facebook page about Melissa, and I know I was meant to read that very message about the connection between you and her. I'm not sure if I'll ever under-stand how things like this happen, but I am truly honored that I get to tell your story, Laney. I hope one day the work that has been done by so many people will bring an ending that may bring a little peace to those that loved you so much until the day you will embrace them all again. Until the day you hug your brother again. Until the day you can celebrate Angie's birthday again. Until the day you can look into the sorrowful eyes of Detective Smith, who tried so hard for so long to solve your case.

As when I started this book, I am writing to you from the patio, and the power of nature is on display again. The rain is falling hard, yet it is a calming rain as if you are talking directly to me from Heaven. Are you telling me through the natural world you are looking down as I write to you? Are you telling me that everything is okay, and you are walking with your mother and father on that eternal beach? That is what I hope you are asking me to tell all, share with all of those who love you, who are still on Earth, who are still waiting for that glorious reunion.

At the beginning of this letter, I quoted the Gospel of Mark. As I have been working through this journey with you, your connection to nature and the river both fit quotes from Mark, and in the river you were found, I have found myself reaching deeper into my understanding of faith, or should I say my faith. As I talk with and about you, I try to find the good in your story. I know how wonderful a person you were and all the people you have had an impact on while you were alive and since your passing. Sometimes, I ask myself, "What does God want me to do with this?" I know from your autopsy that you had a faint, faded tattoo of "MARK" on your ankle. Many who know you best did not know the meaning of the tattoo, but many believed it was possibly for a fallen friend. Knowing you, I would say that is probably true. But could there be another meaning? While contemplating this out loud to my youngest daughter, she mentioned to me that many people, especially young people trying to find their way, often place faith-based chapters and verses somewhere on their bodies to remind them of a higher power.

We will never know the true reason for that small, faint work of art, but I want to believe that it eventually brought you peace and into the arms of the Almighty. Was the tattoo's meaning important to the fact that you were found in the calm part of the angry river? Was the "MARK" on your ankle the Gospel of Mark, telling the story of John the Baptist, baptizing those who came forth to the river Jordan? Was there a higher power that lifted you from the banks of that river and into the calm center of the waters so that you would be found? I now believe the body is a vessel for the soul and when we pass our soul will be lifted up into the heavens. I am pretty sure you must have been scared that night as that evil-hearted person squeezed the life out of your body, but I also believe that God opened his arms for you and whispered in your ear, "Everything is okay."

The individual that took you from your family and friends

probably saw a different vision that night, and that, I hope, is haunting them every single day. One day, that wolf will have to shed the sheep's clothing to answer to his maker. One day, hopefully while they are still here on Earth, they will have searched for forgiveness and take responsibility for that night. Until then, we will keep asking questions until we have an answer. We will keep the pressure on. It may take another twenty-five years for that to happen, but I truly believe one day it will.

As you have looked over my shoulder while I was writing this book, I hope you have seen that your presence here on Earth was not forgotten. Your family and friends have been reaching out to tell your story to anyone who will listen. They have created Facebook pages to allow people to see who you were. They hope that one day someone will see that page and say, "I know what happened," then step forward to express what they know. The funny thing about your Facebook page is that it is kind of an old social media platform, but it is perfect for people close to our age—my age and the age you would have been. The reason I say it is funny is that I believe if you were still here, you would be a social media sweetheart.

You would have shined in the social media world, whether it was making fun of how you were aggravating your kids or making hilarious country music dance videos with your friends. Your smile and fun-loving attitude would have lit up the screens of all your friends' phones and of many who didn't even know you. You would have been posting the proud moments of your son's or daughter's graduation and the birth of your first grandchild. You would be uploading family vacation pictures with your brother David and with your niece and nephew. The celebrations of birthdays, anniversaries, weddings, and over-served nights out on the town with your friends would fill the photo section of Facebook and Instagram. You would send out that sentimental "I love you" to your loving mother and father, who would have preceded you with their passing. Who knows? With the reemergence of line dancing and old country music bands, we could have actually met at the Diamond Rio concert here in town where Angie and I ran into each other. Maybe we would have taken an Instagram picture. I know you would have been someone people loved to follow.

In reality, you and I probably would have never met. Your story would be a happy one with the accomplishments of many dreams. You might have been famous or you might have been perfectly okay with a modest life and not much attention. Well, I'm sure your friends would disagree with the attention part, but you get know what I mean.

I also wouldn't have gotten to know David and his family. I wouldn't know Angie, Joy, Brittany, or Karrie. I wouldn't have gotten to talk to Frank Smith and become friends with the intense yet soft-hearted man who spent the last six years of his career chasing every lead he could to find the person who took you from this Earth. I wouldn't have spoken to Mark Reiber or Scott Thomas to learn what it takes to do an investigation. I wouldn't have met Dustin Foul and been able to tell his story of redemption, or make a friend with Mike Sturgeon. I wouldn't have started the Cold Case MHS program and been able to help others who have similar stories that need to be told.

I am beginning to see why our paths have crossed. You wanted to help others from Heaven. You wanted to bring light to dark stories that haven't been told. You are the guardian angel who has pushed me to do more and to start a movement to bring some peace to others.

While here on Earth, your life wasn't necessarily perfect, but it was perfectly yours. You had your own style, soft-hearted, humorous, and kind, yet you were a bit of a hard-ass when needed. You could sit with a friend in need all night long or jump in front of a punch to stop someone from hurting someone else. Like most of us, you loved your family but sometimes wanted to spend time away from them. You had a look that killed, no irony intended, whether it was professionally or a night on the town. At twenty-three, you were doing what people that age do: having fun. From what I gather from your friends, you were fun, unpredictable, and maybe even a bit wild. One thing I did learn from them was that you were planning a future. The professional world was going to see someone who would rise to the top, while having a family was definitely a goal as well.

As I sit here writing about you, I see so many of those characteristics in my own daughters. Strong women striving to live life to the fullest. I also become extremely heartbroken knowing that your parents never got to see the many chapters of your life. I know your friends often sit back and laugh at the way you commanded the room and made things exciting in many ways. I also know they sit and cry knowing what you could have become. While driving one day, I heard Hardy's song "Give Heaven Some Hell," and immediately texted Karrie that I couldn't help but think of you when I heard the words. From what everyone has told me, the line "you had a wild side but you had amazing grace" seems to fit you so well.

One day, you and your friends will meet again and do that line dancing you were all so good at. You will laugh, cry, and enjoy the eternal party that will happen when they all get there to join you. You will hold your brother again, and the whole family will be back together. You will be able to say "thank you" to Frank Smith and all of those who worked on your case. Oh, and one day I will finally get to meet you. One day, we will all see the "Spirit Like a Dove" descend upon us, and you will be right there to welcome us home.

Until then, you keep a watch over your family and friends. You whisper in the ears of those of us trying to tell your story, and you know justice will be served one day.

Sincerely,


RANDY

# Epilogue - Six Degrees

**"Six degrees of separation is the theory that any person on the planet can be connected to any other person on the planet through a chain of acquaintances that has no more than five intermediaries."**
— Paul Kirvan, Techtarget.com

"Six Degrees of Separation" is a concept often used in conversations about weird occurrences that may show up in life. I feel that most of us use this idea in the wrong context of its true meaning. As a matter of fact, most of us have never really looked it up to see where this comes from; we simply use it as a figure of speech when things seem a bit strange. Well, I decided if I'm going to use this, I better know the true meaning of the words and whether it was a real scientific phenomenon or something someone made up to sound intelligent. I didn't look this up because I was bored; I have stated in this book several times I feel there was some reason Laney was brought into my life. One question kept creeping back into my head every time I looked at her picture or started to dive into the case again: Why me?

I discovered that "Six Degrees of Separation" has been tested over and over again, from sending letters from California to New York, to a person the original experimental group did not know through friends, to finally get the letter to that person, to businesses using it to connect concepts to improve their outcomes. This theory seems to have strong evidence to support its reality. It's a strange concept to imagine, but as things progressed in our quest to find more out about Laney, it seemed like the link between her and me was strangely close. Again, I felt that bizarre feeling I was chosen for this case, rather than merely picking it randomly.

As far as my "Six Degrees of Separation" to Laney, the first connection is obviously the tie to my hometown of Fairfield, Ohio. Fairfield has had its share of weird things happen during its history, but murder is not very high on that list. As time would pass, that would change a bit, but many towns go through that as dynamics in the area change. It still doesn't have the big-city crime reputation, but Fairfield is not the same safe, sleepy town of the 1980s. I guess the real draw for me was where Laney was last seen. It was a place of fond memories from my childhood. It was a place my parents would hang out with their friends to bowl, while I used the time to make friends and enjoy the arcade games in the lobby. For such a beautiful girl to go missing from somewhere that was such a happy place for me was a dark spot in the middle of a joyous picture of my past. How could this happen in my hometown? That isn't exactly the epitome of the six degrees rule, but it was a link that could not be denied.

I had never met Laney and was quite a bit older than her, so thinking we had any connection was far from my mind. When I saw her picture on that website I thought, *What a shame she is no longer around to share her beauty.* The pictures used on websites, billboards, and news articles always showed her with such a wonderful smile. It was one that would draw you in immediately. Plus, the fact that I had two beautiful daughters of my own that were close to the age when Laney died really hit me hard. But truly, what are the chances we were linked in any way? It had to be zero. I assumed I would be talking with people completely out of my circle with their stories to describe the Laney Gwinner they knew.

When talking with Karrie, she mentioned how she and Laney were introduced to each other by Shad and EJ. As the conversation progressed, Karrie talked about how the girls in their group would get together and venture to different locations, following the rodeo fellas around. In the middle of the discussion, she told me that a set of brothers who were big in the rodeo world knew EJ and may have some insight into who he was and possibly how he could be related to Laney's case. "The brothers that run a bull-riding farm out East, Kenny McElroy and—"

I interrupted her to say, "Wait. Who did you just mention?"

"Kenny McElroy, the owner of K Bar C Bucking Bulls."

A bit startled, I jumped in with, "Big guy, goatee mustache, funny fella?"

"Yes, that's him!" she exclaimed.

Then I blurted out, "I know him! He's one of my great friends!"

I had not met Karrie before we started talking, at least not formally, but we did have an interaction when I was a senior in high school. We had won the state championship in football and did a tour of all the other schools in the district, like we had won the Super Bowl. Karrie, much younger than I, was a seventh grader at the time, and she remembered us coming to her classroom to celebrate with them. Did I actually talk to Karrie or high-five her? I don't know, but we at least had crossed paths in a way. For her to mention a great friend of mine was a surprise, to say the least. He had been my assistant and had coached my oldest daughter in soft-ball from 2000 to 2003.

After, I talked to other friends and family that Evan and I thought might have information about Laney. When we called the detective initially placed on her case, we found him working in the Clerk of Courts office in Fairfield, Ohio. Sergeant Ed Roberts, his rank when Laney went missing, responded to my email and invited me to visit with him to talk about her case. He said he would be glad to talk with us, but he prefaced it with, "I can't comment too much because I'm no longer on the force, and it is still an open case." Evan and I responded that we understood the situation. As we entered his office, after going through metal detectors and getting strange looks by the officer checking us through, Ed stared at me inquisitively for a moment, then asked me, "Are you Ben Hubbard's son?"

Thinking he knew my father from his days as a teacher, admin-istrator, and football coach at Fairfield High School, I said, "Yes, I am."

He asked, kind of like a detective, "Did you play Babe Ruth baseball for Oscar Messer?"

A bit perplexed, I answered, "I did."

He smiled a bit and asked, "Do you remember me?"

Thinking in my head, *Shit, you are going to look bad if you say no*, I sheepishly had to tell him I could not remember.

He stated with a smile, "You played second base and centerfield for me on that baseball team." Ed had been the assistant coach for my Babe Ruth team. It came back to me, and I remembered him showing up to practice in his uniform or watching him leave early because something happened and he was called to duty. Another connection. Laney reintroduced me to one of my childhood mentors and brought back some wonderful memories.

The connections to Laney were just beginning, but I was really starting to think this couldn't be an accident. It seemed there was something beyond myself that was pulling Laney and me together.

Evan and I continued speaking to her friends over the phone, and I felt we were all getting closer. I asked them one day if we could all meet for dinner someday to put faces with names and talk about Laney and her case. They all agreed. I picked a pizza place close to all of us and anxiously set a time to meet. It was one of the best moments of this whole experience. We all hugged and introduced ourselves then got to talking about Laney.

At one point, Angie looked at me and asked, "Haven't we met before?"

Thinking hard, I responded, "I don't think so."

She told me she swore we had met and I looked like someone she knew. She asked if I did anything with baseball, like coaching. I told her no, but my brother did for a long time. I said that he and I look a lot alike, so maybe she'd met him. Then she said that her cousin played for Hamilton High School and pitched in the Cincinnati Reds minor league system for the Dayton Dragons. She stated, "My cousin, Curtus Moak, was a pitcher for the Dragons and—"

I immediately interrupted her and said, "What is your cousin's name?"

She tilted her head as if I'd really caught her attention, then repeated, "Curtus Moak."

I said, "Wait a minute, that's my cousin!" My mother's maiden name was Norinne Moak. Wow! One of Laney's best friends is actually a distant relative of mine. This was getting stranger by the day. This could not be happening by accident.

The six degrees wouldn't stop. Mark Reiber, the retired detective I have been referencing in this book, was another strange connection. Mark played football for my father and played on the same team with my brother at Lockland High School back in 1974. I was only six years old at the time and didn't know Mark then, but, as I previously described, I got a strange email from him in 2019. He reached out and said he had emailed me a year prior, but I did not answer. I did not get that email because he actually forgot to hit send. He could have let it go, but he didn't. He tried again, but I wasn't sure what his interest in Laney's case was until he told me that he had moved into the Gwinners' old home. This couldn't be a coincidence. A man I didn't know but was connected through my family became a detective, retired, then moved into the house of a woman who was killed, and now we were both working together to find her killer. This couldn't be real.

The strange connections continued into my classroom. I was discussing Laney's case with my forensic science classes and how we were searching for anything that may turn the case around. I mentioned I was looking for one of her bosses at the time of her disappearance. The next week we had parent-teacher conferences, and one parent signed up to come see me. This was unusual, since most of my students were upperclassmen and my class was an elective, so normally I had no parents attend these meetings. When the parent walked in, she told me she really didn't come to see me about her son's performance in class. She wanted to talk to me about the case I was working on, the Laney Gwinner case.

She said she heard I was looking for Laney's boss and that she knew him. I said, "Really? Can you tell me who he is?"

She responded with, "He's my ex-husband." What were the chances that I had the son of a woman in my class who used to be married to the man I was in search of?

These connections continued with Aby Overbay, who I mentioned in Chapter 4. Aby was a student of mine in 2005, thirteen years prior to me even looking into Laney's case. Recently, another student of mine, Aydin, was in my cold-case class. He went home to his parents to tell them what we were doing and that I had been researching Laney's case for years. The next day, I got an email from his mother stating that she was an acquaintance of Laney's. She told me the story of how she went to the vigil for Laney right after her disappearance and while she was there she met a young man. They began to date and later would go on to get married and have a baby boy they named Aydin. I thought to myself, *This has to be a joke.*

Through this journey to find Laney's killer, I have found a distant relative. I had similar friends as Laney's. I had a student who spent hours with Laney every day for several years. I was connected to a detective who moved into Laney's old house. I had a student in my class whose mother was married to Laney's boss at the time of her death. And I had a student who was born because his mother and father met at a vigil for Laney's disappearance.

I am convinced that Laney has been guiding us for all of these years, and she felt it was the right time to bring us together. She has been orchestrating the process to link us all together for one reason: Laney knew we would not stop looking until we found the answer and that, along the way, we would help others keep hope alive in their own tragic stories of loss.

It is normal that people you know change your life, but it is rare that someone you never knew could have such a profound effect on it. I truly believe Laney has made me a better person just from that one act of my looking up her name one day. She led me to start a new class that is designed to help others. She has led me to challenge myself to be more empathetic toward others who have suffered great loss. She has made me appreciative of my new relationships and cherish my older ones more. She has led me to love my family more and to hold on to every moment we have on this Earth.

Alana "Laney" Gwinner's legacy will live on forever, and one day the wolf will be stripped of his lamb's clothing and exposed to the world. I would like the killer to know that the six degrees of separation will one day bring you to light. A person who knows a person who knows you will come forward with information you may have let slip to yet another person. We are all connected by less than six people, and one day that one person who is only six steps away from you will tell the truth.

# Acknowledgments

Thank you to my beautiful wife Sherri for her unconditional support for all the different things I take on in my life, from coaching sports, to spending our cash on science projects for class, to writing a book. Thank you for pushing me to finish this book. I often would get easily distracted, but you were there to reel me in and get me back on track. Your continued support through the good times and the rough times in life is something I cherish each and every day. I love you with all my heart.

To my kids, Macy and Meg, thank you for always listening to my stories and acting like you were interested in all of them. You both make me so proud to be your dad. Whether it was on the sidelines or in the classroom, your constant support is a treasure I will hold on to for life. Macy, thank you for listening to my podcasts; I know that most of the listeners are you listening more than once. Way to boost my ego. Meg, thank you for helping start this process of looking into Laney's case and following along with our progress to this point—and beyond. Your ideas were many, and I promise I used some of them.

As mentioned in my dedication, I was hoping to finish this book before my parents passed away, but unfortunately, I was not able to do that. I hope they are looking down today knowing I finished what I had started. This was always a must in our family. Mom and Dad instilled in me that accomplishments can only be achieved if you finish what you started, and I thank them so much for those lessons. Hopefully, God will give you some time to read the book in Heaven. If you see Laney, tell her I am trying to bring her killer to justice. I love you, Mom and Dad, and I miss you so much.

To my siblings, thank you for setting examples along the way. You have been a major part of all things I have done in my life. Even though it wasn't always easy, we always had each other's backs, and I truly appreciate and love each of you.

Evan Fletcher, thank you for inspiring me to do more. You came into my classroom and into my life at exactly the right time. Your inquisitive nature and your no-fear attitude sparked something in me to be better at my job as a teacher and to continue learning every day. I learned a tremendous amount from you as we went through this journey together. You taught this old dog some new tricks, and I am forever grateful.

Angela, Karrie, Joy, and Brittany, thank you for opening up to Evan and me about Laney. Without you, I would not have known who Laney really was. She would have merely been a name in an article or a newscast, but you made me feel as if I knew her. Over the years, we have built a friendship and a bond that will last forever. I hope this book honors Laney the way you would want her to be honored. Through your guidance and the love I know you share for Laney, we have at least brought her story back into the light. Hopefully, one day soon you will all see justice for Laney.

David Gwinner, you are an amazing man. I know when we have spoken it has not been easy for you. You let me into a part of your life that I still cannot truly imagine. I hope through this book you can see how many people Alana has touched, from those who knew her to those, like me, who never had a chance to be in her presence. Your mom, dad, and sister are all smiling down on you and your family, watching over each of you until the day you will all join together again.

To LaDonna Humphrey, I want to say thank you for answering my emails and phone calls nearly six years ago. From the moment we spoke, I knew we would get along. When I mentioned I wanted to write a book, which I had never done before, you quickly got on the phone to help me out. You have been a guiding force through this whole process, and your support is greatly appreciated. Thank you for believing in me and introducing me to Leya and Steven Booth from Genius Book Publishing. It took some guts to do that because I could have been really bad at this.

Sheryl "Mac" McCollum, you are a true inspiration to me. You always make time to answer my texts or phone calls with my really naïve questions, and I truly appreciate all that you have done for me. From the first phone call about starting the Cold Case Program here at Mason High School, to calling my assistant principal, I think while you were on your way to a scene, to reassure her that we could do this program safely, you have always been in my corner. Your expertise, along with your genuine warm heart, is something people need to know about you. You do your job for the right reasons: not for the glamor, but to bring justice to those who cannot speak for themselves.

To Scott Thomas, Mark Reiber, and Chad Jones, thank you for giving me an education like no other. All three of you have served our communities with pride by wearing the blue uniform, and I salute you. I also want to thank each of you for walking me through the process and giving me ideas of what to do next. Your insight into the criminal world has been very enlightening. You allowed me to share my ideas even if some of them were off the wall, then you straightened me out and brought me back down to Earth. I have learned so much from each of you, and I hope to keep working with you for a long time.

Thank you to all my colleagues at Mason High School for the last twenty-two years of my career. I want to especially thank Kurt Dinan and Michelle Bruewer for taking time to edit and walk me through the book-writing process. English was not my major, and I would say they both would agree.

To Leya and Steven Booth, thank you for taking a chance on me. I have never tried to do something like this, and it takes some guts to give a guy like me this opportunity. You have been patient with me, considering this book was supposed to be completed a long time ago. I truly appreciate all you have done for me. I know Leya will be glad she doesn't have to edit my awful grammar anymore.

To the students and athletes I have encountered over the past thirty-four years, I want to say thank you for all the great memories. To all of my Cold Case MHS students, you have been an inspiration to me for the hard work you have done over the past six years to bring light back to stories that have fallen into the darkness. I also want to say thank you for making me try to be the best I could be in my job. Teaching and coaching has been a blessing. because of all the relationships I have built over the years. I hope that you learned something from me, because I definitely learned so much from all of you. My career has been tremendous because of the wonderful people I have been around for all of these years.

Other acknowledgments:

Jessica Schmidt with FOX19News WXIX, Frank Smith, Alex Campbell, Rick Baughman, Shanna Bumiller, Doyle Burke, James Carsten, Mason High School administration, Dustin Faul, Kevin Gannon, Detective Stephen Hickey, Detective John Thompson, Dr. Mark Godsey, Stephanie Harlowe, Angeline Hartmann, Brad Johansen, David Kash, Shayla Klein, Kaylie Levine, the late Todd Matthews, Melissa Morgan, Aby Overbay, Christine Pelisek, Sgt. Darrell Price, Ken Purcell, Kirk Reinhart, Brian and Glen Roth,

Captain Kevin Savage, Lt. Kris Shultz, Mike Sturgeon, Dr. Gary Utz, Karin Johnson with WLWT Channel 5, Kenny McElroy, Steven Burkhardt, Kimberly Kelley, Ed Roberts, Marci Hammond, and everyone else who has given their time to help with this process.

# Appendix

Cases in the Dark that were brought back into the light by Cold Case MHS

# Alana "Laney" Gwinner
## (STARTED 2018)

Laney disappeared on December 10, 1997 from Gilmore Bowling Lanes in Fairfield, OH after a night of celebration with a friend. She was found in the Ohio River January 11, 1998. Cause of death ruled asphyxiation. **Unsolved.**

# Cheryl Thompson
## (MHS CLASS OF 2022)

Cheryl disappeared from downtown Cincinnati in March of 1998. Her naked body was found on the banks of the Little Miami River near Loveland, Ohio two weeks later. **SOLVED! Serial Killer Ralph Howell was identified as the killer.**

# Angela Marie Steele
## (MHS CLASS OF 2021)

On June 4, 1999, Angela's car was found as a staged car accident in Wyandot County, OH with her deceased body inside. Her car was set on fire by an accelerant, but blunt force trauma to the head was the cause of death. **Unsolved.**

# Buffy Jo Freeman
## (MHS CLASS OF 2021)

Buffy's body was found in a park in Springfield, OH on July 12, 2007. She was badly beaten and left to die. Unfortunately, her injuries were compounded by the fact a police officer did not see her body and ran over her with his cruiser. **Unsolved.**

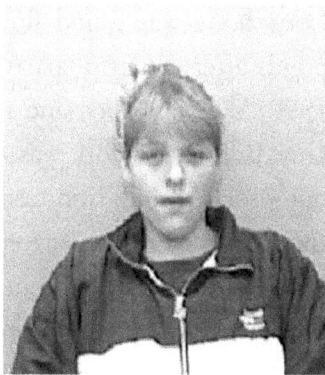

## Lesa Buckley
### (MHS CLASS OF 2022)

Lesa's body was found floating in a pond after a farm party in July 1990. She was raped and murdered. Guy Billy Lee Scott was convicted but proclaims his innocence. Ohio Innocence Project agrees. New DNA tests are currently being processed. **Outcome unknown.**

# Daniel Trautman
## (MHS CLASS OF 2022)

Daniel's body was found in a farm field outside of Columbus, OH on October 29, 2005. He was a recovering alcoholic who was last seen with two men at a bar. Police say his skull was crushed, but he was not killed at the location his body was found. **Unsolved.**

# Liz Falco
## (MHS CLASS OF 2022)

Liz's body was found in a wetland park near the Philadelphia, PA airport on November 14, 1990. She was last seen riding her bike. Her body was covered with a plastic bag and the bike was found several miles away. **Unsolved.**

## Wendy Burkey
### (MHS CLASS OF 2022)

Wendy's body was found on May 26, 2001 lying outside the driver's side door of her work van in the company parking lot. She was shot twice and left to die. **Unsolved.**

# Fame Cooper
## (MHS CLASS OF 2022)

Fame's body was found in a wooded area in Fairmont, WV in July 1990. She was strangled by some type of cord and dragged by an offroad-type vehicle. **Unsolved.**

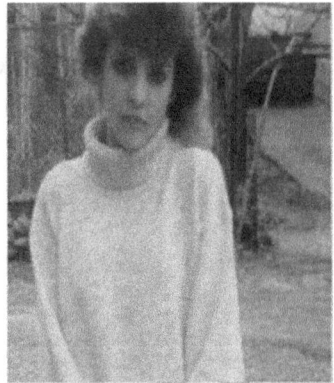

# Bobbie Lee Wells
## (MHS CLASS OF 2022)

Bobbie lived in Michigan, but her body was found wrapped up, lying in a ditch in Fulton County, OH sometime 1980. She had been beaten with a blunt forced object. **Unsolved.**

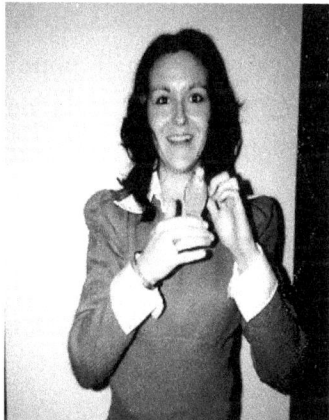

# Regina Hicks
## (MHS CLASS OF 2022)

Regina's body was found in her vehicle in a small pond near her home in Willard, OH on October 22, 2001. She had been missing since October 18, 2001. The cause of death was drowning, but evidence also showed trauma to her head and other parts of her body. **Unsolved.**

# Chelsea Johnson
## (MHS CLASS OF 2021)

Chelsea, a 15-year-old, was found stabbed to death in a small Creek behind her apartment complex on April 15, 2012. She was last seen with an adult male earlier that day. **Unsolved.**

# Amy Hooper
## (MHS CLASS OF 2021)

Amy was found in her apartment in Columbus, OH on March 9, 1992, badly beaten and possibly sexually assaulted. Currently, new information may be moving this case in the right direction. **Unsolved.**

## Pricilla Dawn Hickman
### (MHS CLASS OF 2021)

Pricilla's body was found beaten, wrapped up in the sheets of her bed, and stuffed into a closet in the back of her trailer on January 15, 2009. A witness stated they saw a male leaving the trailer, but he was never found. **Unsolved.**

## David Hadaway
### (MHS CLASS OF 2020)

On July 21, 1986, David was found in a dumpster on the campus of Ohio State University. His body was mutilated and stabbed even after death. Authorities believe David knew his killer or killers. **Unsolved.**

# Alicia Jackson
## (MHS CLASS OF 2021)

Alicia was found stabbed to death in her apartment on December 2, 2010 with her two-year-old son sitting next to her in a highchair. Authorities believe her killer could be a woman. **Unsolved.**

# Erica Fraysure
## (MHS CLASS OF 2020)

Erica went missing on October 21, 1997, after leaving a local video rental store in Bracken County, KY. Her car was found abandoned in a local farm field, but Erica has never been located. **Missing, presumed deceased.**

# Martha Oelman
## (MHS CLASS OF 2020)

Martha was found lying face down, naked on her bed, in Sugar Creek Township, Ohio on September 7, 1997. She had been deceased between 24-48 hours before being found by friends. **Unsolved**.

# Erica Baker
## (MHS CLASS OF 2021)

Ten-year-old Erica was riding her bike near a park in Dayton, Ohio on February 7, 1999, but would never return home. Christian Gabriel admitted to hitting her with a van and then burying her body. Unfortunately, he led police on a wild goose chase to a location where her body was not found. To this day her body is still missing. **Death SOLVED; the whereabouts of her body is still unsolved.**

# Nancy Theobald
## (MHS CLASS OF 2020)

Nancy's partially naked, decomposing body was found in a creek near West Chester, Ohio on December 26, 1977. She had been missing since November of 1977, after leaving her work in downtown Cincinnati. Nancy is most likely a victim of Ralph Howell, a possible serial killer who died in a motor vehicle accident in 1984.

# Lena Ranford
## (MHS CLASS OF 2020)

Lena was a single mother found by elementary students walking to school in an alley in Cincinnati, Ohio on September 23, 1999. Lena had fought her attacker and DNA evidence was collected. As of today, no match has been found. **Unsolved.**

## Rachael Johnson
### (MHS CLASS OF 2020)

On March 30, 1991, Rachael disappeared from Dan Street in Akron,
OH. Later that day she was found
stabbed, sexually assaulted, and
partially burned on Weller Avenue
in Akron. On July 28, 2023, Dan
Rees pleaded guilty to her murder
and waived his right to a jury trial.
**SOLVED**.

# Karen Spencer
## (MHS CLASS OF 2020)

Karen was last seen on December 29, 1989 walking on I-275 near Loveland, Ohio after arguing with her soon-to-be sister-in-law. Witnesses said she was picked up in a reddish-orange truck or car. Karen has not been seen since. **Missing, presumed deceased.**

# Katelyn Markham
## (MHS CLASS OF 2021)

Katelyn disappeared from Fairfield in August 2011. Her body was later found skeletonizcd in a wooded area in Indiana. Her fiancé, John Carter, pleaded guilty to manslaughter in 2024. **SOLVED!**

## Lisa Ann Gross
### (MHS CLASS OF 2020)

On May 21, 2001, Lisa was found with a puncture wound in the back of her head in the bathtub of her home in Delaware County, Ohio, with the water running and strangely covered in shredded paper from the home. **Unsolved.**

## Patti Ann Adkins
### (MHS CLASS OF 2021)

Patti supposedly packed a bag to go on a trip with her married boyfriend. She was told to leave her phone at home. Patti has never been seen since leaving work in Marysville, Ohio, June 29, 2001. **Missing, presumed deceased.**

# Anita Taylor
## (MHS CLASS OF 2021)

Anita Taylor was found by her husband bludgeoned in her home on October 29, 1966. Her one-year-old son was also beaten and left in his crib to die, but he survived. He is still seeking answers to his mother's murder to this day. **Unsolved**.

## Lisa Pruett
### (MHS CLASS OF 2021)

On September 14, 1990, 16-year-old Lisa was found in the backyard of a home in Shaker Heights, Ohio, stabbed 21 times. A young man was indicted and taken to trial, but he was acquitted of her murder. **Unsolved.**

# Amy Mehalivic
## (MHS CLASS OF 2021)

Amy, a 10-year-old student in Bay Village, Ohio was abducted by a man witnesses described to be in his 30s. He used a ruse of helping her buy her mother a gift for a recent job promotion, but on October 27, 1989 Amy would go missing until a jogger found her body in a farm field in February of 1990. **Unsolved**.

# Jeffrey Risner
## (MHS CLASS OF 2023)

Jeffrey, a 6'0", nearly 250 pound man was found stabbed and beaten to death in his detached garage in Fostoria, Ohio on March 2, 2006. Police do not think it was a sneak attack, but still do not have answers. **Unsolved**.

# Chris DeArmond
## (MHS CLASS OF 2023)

Chris was shot to death in the barbershop he worked in the morning of March 17, 2012. Chris was a mentor and often gave kids in need free haircuts. It appears the suspect may have been involved in a feud with some of Chris' family. In 2023 his ex-wife was also murdered, possibly by the same man, who is currently waiting for a trial. Chris' murder is **Unsolved.**

# Brian Schaffer
## (MHS CLASS OF 2023)

Brian was a very successful medical student at Ohio State University. On the night of April 1, 2006, he went out to have some fun at the local college bars. Images caught Brian entering an establishment, but he was never seen leaving. To this day Brian has not returned home. **Missing, presumed deceased.**

# Kareem Brogdon
## (MHS CLASS OF 2023)

Kareem was a man struggling with his demons as an addict. On November 26, 2002, while sitting on the stoop of his apartment complex, someone opened fire. As he tried to flee, the assailant shot him in the back. In the darkness of night, the suspect disappeared. **Unsolved**.

## Ernestine Hurt
### (MHS CLASS OF 2023)

On June 24, 1982, Ernestine was killed by a surprise attack at a bus stop in downtown Cincinnati, Ohio. A witness from far away saw a tall, thin male run from the scene, but it was dark and no other descriptions could be made. **Unsolved**.

# Harry W. Smith
## (MHS CLASS OF 2023)

Harry was known as "Grandpa Walmart" for his warm greeting and grandpa-like smile. He was loved dearly by all who knew him in Chillicothe, Ohio. On October 16, 2011, intruders broke into his home, restrained him, and then killed him with a blow to the back of his head. In an attempt to cover up any evidence they tried to set the house on fire, but passers-by were able to put out the fire. **Unsolved.**

## Judy Martins
### (MHS CLASS OF 2023)

Judy was last seen walking home from a costume party at Kent State University, wearing a red wig. She never made it home and has not been seen since May 24, 1978. **Missing, presumed deceased.**

## Joanne Herbert
### (MHS CLASS OF 2023)

Joanne, 14 years old, was last seen July 23, 1981 at a local store where she had traveled to on her orange bike. Witnesses saw her on the phone, but she would not be seen again until a squirrel hunter found her body in a wooded field, less than three miles from her home, in September of 1981. She had been hit with a blunt object on her head. **Unsolved.**

## Heidi Bake
(MHS CLASS OF 2023)

On June 11, 2010, Heidi was caught in the crossfire of an apparent drug-related robbery. No one heard or saw anything except for her boyfriend who said he was hit on the head with a gun when the gun went off, hitting Heidi. **Unsolved.**

# Robin Durrer

Robin was 19 years old when she was last seen riding her bike on September 10, 1981, in Franklin County, Ohio. Her body was found the next day beside some railroad tracks. She had been sexually assaulted and beaten around the head and neck area. **Unsolved.**

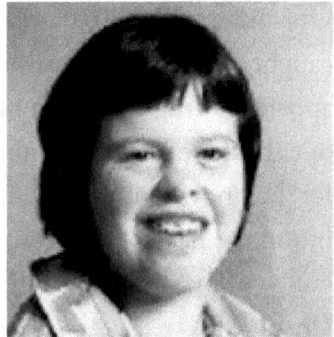

# Asha Degree
## (MHS CLASS OF 2021)

Asha was 9 years old when she packed her bookbag for school in the early morning of February 14, 2000. The unusual part was that she was seen walking along a rural highway in a severe rainstorm, in Shelby, NC. She has not been seen since. Her bookbag would be found several months later in a construction site. Recent work by the FBI has found a vehicle that may have been involved with her disappearance. **Unsolved.**

## Leiksha Streety
### (MHS CLASS OF 2023)

Leiksha was found partially naked, stabbed, and strangled in her downtown Cincinnati apartment on March 10, 2006. The suspect poured Clorox on her and seemed to have spent some time in the apartment before leaving her to be found. **Unsolved.**

## Raymond Wells
### (MHS CLASS OF 2023)

Raymond was a young man trying to change his life. He had enlisted in the Army to get away from his gang affiliation, but he was brutally stabbed in a vehicle and dumped on the road in a quiet cul-de-sac on June 28, 1999. The suspect(s) hit Raymond with their car and dragged him nearly 50 feet. **Unsolved.**

## Devan Duniver
### (MHS CLASS OF 2023)

Devan was six years old when, on June 27, 1997, someone brutally stabbed her and left her in a grassy area where kids were known to play. A 12-year-old boy was arrested and found guilty but was later released based on a possible coerced confession. Dogs followed a scent to a local home, but evidence was not found to connect that person to the case. **Unsolved.**

## Angela Hanaway
### (MHS CLASS OF 2023)

Angela had fallen into a life of addiction. Angela was one of many women found in the Springfield, Ohio area who may have run into the same person or persons. Angela's body was found on June 6, 2008 in a nearby river with evidence of severe physical violence. **Unsolved.**

# Beverly Ann Jarosz
## (MHS CLASS OF 2021)

16-year-old Beverly was found dead by her father on December 28, 1964. She had been stabbed, strangled, and left to die in her upstairs bedroom of their Garfield Heights home. Beverly also had an unknown stalker who had called her the day she was murdered. **Unsolved**.

# Tonia Aldrich
## (MHS CLASS OF 2020)

Tonia was last seen on March 29, 1997 walking along the road after being at a bar in Elyria, OH. Tonia would never be seen again. Her purse and ID were found later, but no evidence was found to indicate what happened to her. **Missing, presumed deceased**.

# Alia Hartman

Alia was a very successful 25-year-old moving up in her job. She was an employee of Tinker Omega, where she had recently been promoted to Assistant Engineer of the Production Department. She truly loved her work and her co-workers. On May 9, 2008, in Springfield, Ohio, Alia's house caught fire and was later determined an arson. As the firefighters finished their initial walk-through after putting the fire out they uncovered Alia's burned body in the rubble. Her killer is still at large. **Unsolved.**

## Stacey Colbert
### (MHS CLASS OF 2024)

Stacey was preparing to go to a conference for her work on March 23, 1998. Stacey did not arrive and concerns began to spiral. When her sister went to her apartment in Columbus, Ohio, she found it a bit in disarray, but this wasn't that unusual for Stacey. The refrigerator door was open and uneaten pizza was found on the table. She was reported missing until her skeletal remains were found in a field 40 miles from her home six years later. **Unsolved.**

## Deanna Perry, Charles Climer, Brianna Smith
### (MHS CLASS OF 2024)

Deanna was known as the mother of the community in Columbus, Ohio. She often opened her house to those who needed a place to stay or food to eat. Unfortunately, she may have let the wrong person in to stay with her. One such person was the mother of Brianna Smith. Brianna was a beautiful one-year-old who Deanna took care of while her mother tried to straighten out her life. Brianna was caught in the wrong place at the wrong time. On October 15, 2010, the house was surrounded with gasoline and Molotov cocktails were thrown onto the porch, setting the house ablaze. Deanna, Brianna, and Charles didn't make it out. **Unsolved.**

Charles Climer - (MHS Class of 2024) - Charles was Deanna Perry's grandson who was in the house when it was set on fire. He tried to escape through a window, then returned to the house to try to reach his grandmother and one-year-old Brianna, but was unsuccessful. **Unsolved.**

# Jennifer Cooke
## (MHS CLASS OF 2024)

In the sleepy town of Grandview Heights, the brutal murder of Jennifer Cooke shook the town. She found in her apartment on August 11, 2013 stabbed multiple times. She was a single mom doing well and moving up in her job. Her car was found two streets over from her home with her purse and identification still in it. **Unsolved.**

# Joan Palacio
## (MHS CLASS OF 2024)

Joan, unfortunately, found herself living a high-risk lifestyle in Toledo, OH. On September 15, 2002, she ran into the wrong person who beat and strangled her to death, then left her body by a dumpster in a vacant lot. **Unsolved.**

# Jillian Miles
## (MHS CLASS OF 2024)

Jillian was a mother of two who was shot in her apartment, in Dayton, Ohio, on February 19, 2013. She came downstairs after taking a shower where she was confronted with a gunman who shot her twice. She was left to die on the living room floor with her two young children in the room. **Unsolved.**

## MacKenzie Branham
### (MHS CLASS OF 2024)

MacKenzie was a beautiful 8-year-old who died in a house fire on April 27, 2006 at the home where her mother and boyfriend were residents in Jeffersonville, Ohio. The fire was ruled an accident at first but was quickly changed to an arson. There were possible signs of some type of sexual assault on MacKenzie, but no assailant has been identified. Her mother and her boyfriend were able to escape the fire, but MacKenzie did not. **Unsolved.**

# Eveline Ashbaugh
## (MHS CLASS OF 2024)

Eveline was a llama farmer in Delaware, Ohio. On May 5, 2007, her farmhand noticed she was not out helping on the farm, so he went to the house to see if she was okay. Unfortunately, she was not. She had been savagely attacked with a knife and stabbed multiple times. An upstairs window screen had been cut and a wooden ladder was found leaning against the house. **Unsolved.**

# Marcia King "The Buckskin Girl"

(MHS CLASS OF 2024)

For nearly 35 years "The Buckskin Girl," who died on April 24, 1981, had been listed as a Jane Doe in Miami County, Ohio. With the hard work of Detective Hickey and a crew of scientists, they were able to use genetic genealogy to identify her as Marcia King from Arkansas. With new technology, evidence found at the scene may soon lead to her killer. **Unsolved, but moving forward.**

## Rebecca Lynn Carroll
### (MHS CLASS OF 2024)

Rebecca was a loving mother, but found her way into a very high-risk lifestyle. On April 7, 2010, her body was found floating in the Big Darby Creek in Columbus, OH. She had been missing for several weeks before her remains were found by kayakers. **Unsolved.**

## Linda Pagano
### (MSH CLASS OF 2024)

Linda was last seen on September 9, 1974, walking away from her stepfather's home in Strongsville, Ohio. She had arrived home after a night out with her boyfriend. It is rumored she had a fight with her stepfather about being out too late. She would remain missing until her skeletonized body was found in February 5, 1975, along the Rocky River in a Cleveland State Park. She had been shot with a small caliber gun. **Unsolved**.

# About the Author

Biology/Chemistry Major in College
Master's Degree in Education Administration
34 years of Teaching
27 years of Coaching multiple sports
Innovative class creations - Forensic Science, In-school Zoo at
Harrison, Cold Case Course

## **Biography**:

With over 34 years of experience in the classroom in the South-western Ohio area, Randy Hubbard is a passionate educator with a reputation for and a deep commitment to inspiring students in both the classroom and on the field. A graduate of Fairfield High School and of Georgetown College, where he earned degrees in biology and chemistry, his knowledge and passion in those fields has leant itself well to his decades of educating others. Randy has combined his scientific background with a love for hands-on learning, creating innovative and engaging courses such as Forensic Science and Cold Case Investigation at William Mason High

School, and the unique in-school zoo at Harrison High School. In the Cold Case course, which he proposed and created, he innovatively educates students to investigate unsolved crimes through podcasting and other unique presentations. Outside of the classroom, he has spent 27 years coaching multiple sports, all the while instilling teamwork, discipline, and leadership in countless young athletes. Through his unforgettable teaching and coaching, Randy has built a lasting legacy of learning. Randy currently resides in Ohio, but will soon enjoy retirement alongside his wife, Sherri, and two children in South Carolina.

www.ingramcontent.com/pod-product-compliance
Lightning Source LLC
Chambersburg PA
CBHW062117020426
42335CB00013B/1001